WASHINGTON !

ARE YOU LISTENING ?

DEATH BRINGS CHANGE TO D.C.

By **Michael G'Francisco**

INTRODUCTION

The Preamble to the United States Government reads: We the people of the United States, in order to form a more perfect Union, establish justice, insure domestic tranquility, provide for the common defense, promote the general welfare, and secure the blessings of liberty to ourselves and our posterity, do ordain and establish this Constitution for the United States of America.

The above was this country's actual introduction, and **does not** assign powers to a FEDERAL GOVERNMENT. It seems that the Founding Father's intentions were to protect people and treat them as equals.

The Pledge Allegiance written in August of 1892, by Francis Bellamy simply states: "I pledge Allegiance to the flag of the United States, and to the REPUBLIC for which it stands, one nation under God, indivisible, with liberty and justice for all."

Francis Bellamy, 1892

A **REPUBLIC** form of government is a political system in which the supreme power lies in a body of citizens **who** can elect people to represent them.

A **DEMOCRACY** is a form of government where the power resides in the right to vote and is exercised by the **free citizen** throughout a system of elected representation.

The problem, no matter how the two terms are defined, is $$$$$. Today, laws are bought and passed by a very small elite group to rule on their behalf. Somewhere along the way, Greed married Power, and an **OLIGARCHY** form of government was created. That is what our government is all about today! A NATION THAT IS RULED BY THE MONEY OF A FEW TO ELECT PEOPLE TO OFFICE!

A quote from history:

"If ever a time should come, when vain and aspiring men shall possess the highest seats in Government, our country will stand in need of its experienced patriots to prevent its ruin."
Samuel Adams (circa 1765)

DISCLAIMER:

This story is pure fiction. All characters appearing in this work are fictitious. Any resemblance to a real person(s), living or dead, is purely coincidental. No one in this book is based on a real person, all characters are entirely fictional.

If the depiction of a certain corporation or government title or position should result in similarities, these similarities were not intended. Names, no matter how similar, are intended to be purely fictional and any connection is strictly un-intended. The exceptions are: The history of Emiliano Zapata, "Poncho" Villa, Francisco Madero and the others involved in the Mexican Revolution.

Author's Note:

This book's contents is pure fiction, except for the references to the story and the names in the Mexican Revolution of 1910. Within its pages are also inserts and quotes of famous people pertaining to certain situations, which are clearly noted.

The book's graphic depictions of murder and mayhem are strictly out of the imagination of an aging author who has lived beyond eighty years and has had to witness his great wonderful country exploited for profit by a few which, has been gained from the blood and sweat of many. This atrocity has been carried out by corrupted government elected officials voting for the intervention around the world to impose the will of the elite few in their quest for power and money. Our government's police actions and covert operations of invading other countries to take down regimes is sheer disrespect for us and the opposing country's citizens and soldiers.

We, the people of this country through our government's laws and regulations, can trade and have business relationships with other nations without attempting to oust another country's leader and give them a false democratic way of life. Mutual agreement or honest negotiations can solve problems without conflict.

This country should not, on one hand, cause a conflict in another country and then respond with military might to overcome what we caused in the first place. It's like setting your neighbor's house on fire and then bringing your water hose to put it out.

America, a country whose land of plenty has benefited it original natives and all those who came after who wished to succeed through hard work and sacrifice, has, over the course of the last fifty years, been steadily violated by the greed for money and power and global control.

Peace on earth can't be achieved if no one takes the time to think what war does to both sides of a conflict. What is left after a conflict are the dead, the maimed soldiers without arms, legs or even worse, the soldiers stressed from the strain of battle, wives without husbands or vice versa, children left without parents and the massive destruction of homes and cities.

It's completely human to protect what he or she processes, but I doubt that a person should fight to protect the elite's desire to obtain more wealth and power. Equality, freedom and the right to live a fruitful life can be obtained without bloodshed.   The marvels of our planet permits anyone to create, grow, build or invent things to earn a profit without greed. History has shown that greed and power has always led to eventual ruin and damnation.

Michael G'Francisco

CONTENTS:

CHAPTER ONE
A NATION IS SHOCKED—Monday, May 5, 2014---9:52 am

Ringgg, ringgg! "Tom Sunday here."

"What's going on in D. C.? This morning's news shocked the world! Every phone in every newsroom all over the country is ringing. Mass murder of government officials. Three Senators, the Speaker of the House and the Secretary of Defense are all assassinated in one hour this morning? It's the St. Valentine's Day Massacre, except there isn't any wall. Wow, Tom that's a lot of murdered people before breakfast."

"Wayne Albrite, how in the hell are you? Long time no hear. How are things in Chi-town? And, to answer your question, you know as much as I do at present."

"Yeah, sure the head of the CIA doesn't know what's going on in the whole wide world. That's a bunch of crap, ol' buddy. As far as Sinatra's 'toddlin' town' the Windy City is becoming the cha-cha capital of the world."

"Look Wayne, we get and follow up all cases, but this one came out of left field. The Feds and my staff are in the pickle barrel together on this one. Really, what the media is dishing out is all anyone has to go on presently. The FBI and my staff are assembling teams as we speak to check each shooting."

"Myself, Vice-President James Thorne, the FBI Director, John W. Domel, General Josh White, the head of the Joint Chiefs of Staff, Todd Gettem, the Attorney General and Edwin Cage with the National Security Affairs are meeting with President Rackston Stone this afternoon at four o'clock in the Situation Room to discuss plans to take whatever actions are necessary to catch this group of assassins or terrorist, if that's the case. I'll get back to you if I can on a secured line to keep you informed, that's if my mouth isn't sealed by the President. Do we have a deal?"

"Hey Tom, we may not be blood related, only bro's by marriage, but we do trust each other. Your decision is fine with me, as long as I get the exclusive on the story's finale."

"Agreed. All any one has at present for the responsibility of these five heinous acts of sniper assassinations is the one word **"Zapata"** which was sent in a single communication to the Associated Press's news media's wire service that read, ***"It begins, Zapata."***

HISTORY OF ZAPATA and PONCHO VILLA

"Yeah, Tom. Say, wasn't that some Mexican hero from the early 1900's?"

"Yes. Emiliano Zapata was the peasant's hero who enlisted the help of Poncho Villa to fight against the injustices done to the Mexican people by President Porfirio Diaz. Zapata was an incorruptible leader of the Mexican peasants. He and his brother Eufemio hooked up with another fighter of freedom, Francisco Poncho Villa, from Northern Mexico to champion the poor Mexican farmer during the 1910 to 1920 Mexican Revolution. All three gave their loyalties to Francisco Madero. If my memory is correct their revolutionary slogan was
'Tierra y Libertad' or in English ***'Land and Liberty'***."

"Sound like a great story. Tom, do you remember the jest of it?"

"I think I do, if you got the time to listen?"

"Sure do, bro, go for it."

"It was basically a battle between the large rich landowners and the poor peasant farmers. Zapata campaigned for the rights of peasants against the wealthy plantation owners who were backed by the dictator Porfirio Daiz. Wayne, it actually isn't much different than today's political scenario of the rich elite ruling our government by the means of election donations. Diaz defeated Francisco Madero in the 1910 election.

"Now, if I can recall correctly, Madero fled Mexico after his defeat to the United States where he declared himself the legitimate President of Mexico. He made arrangements to have Zapata and Villa unite their efforts to retake Mexico City while he remain in the United States out of harm's way.

"In 1911, Madero returned and a terrible six day battle ensued to take the town of Cuautla. The collapse off the town caused Diaz to resign and leave Mexico for Europe probably with bulging pockets. This made Madero the provisional President of Mexico.

"But Wayne, the story has a sad ending. Madero tried to buy off Zapata with land and money. Zapata was insulted and refused. You see, Zapata, Villa and Madero had originally devised a plan whereas all the people of Mexico were too share equally in the spoils of their victory.

| "Poncho" Villa | Zapata | Francisco Madero |

"Madero was assassinated in 1913 by his own General Victoriano Huerta who took over the country. Huerta wanted to unite his army with Zapata's army, Zapata would have no part in it.

| General Victoriano Huerta | Venustiano Carranza | Eulalio Gutierrez |

"Without Zapata's and Villa's aid, Huerta fearing for his life, fled the country. What followed was a popular moderate politician, Venustiano Carranza, who also had organized an army to help overthrow Huerta, called a meeting with Zapata and Villa. He wanted to appoint himself the President of Mexico, but Zapata and Villa wanted General Eulalio Gutierrez to be president. Carranza rejected their choice.

"The battle over control of Mexico continued and Emiliano Zapata (real name Doroteo Arango) was ambused and assassinated on April 4, 1919. It took four more years to kill the Mexican 'Robin Hood' Villa. He was assassinated July 20, 1923."

"Wow, Tom you sure know your history. But, now back to reality. What is the government going to do about the present killers of these five elected and appointed officials?"

"Wayne, that's the big question of the day. I guess the first place to start is in the names and positions of those who were killed. Is there a connection, will it tell us something or give us a lead to follow? The moment you hung up I'm going to begin listing their names, positions and how they met their end to see if I can find a connection. It might provide me a reason for these assassinations. Can't do much more until I get the five authopsy reports."

CHAPTER TWO
NAMES/TITLES OF THOSE ASSASSINATED

While waiting for the autopsy reports, I began to gather information. There wasn't a clesr reason why these men were assassinated.

1. **Senator Howard Lange,** (R-TN) Chairman of the Committee of Energy & Natural Resources and four other committees. He was taken out by a sniper at 08:37 hours while on his regular morning jog on his estate grounds in Howie, Maryland. The shooter didn't take out his bodyguard jogging a short distant behind him.
2. **Arthur Thurston,** (R-W.V.) Speaker of the House. He was shot at 08:42 hours by a sniper on route to his workout gym adjacent to his estate home in Charley Town, West Virginia. He was alone.
3. **Senator Abe Wines**, (R-WY) Chairman of the Committee of Foreign Affairs and four other Committees. He was sniper shot at 08:49 hours while horse backing riding with his wife on their ranch near Baramie, Wyoming. The sniper spared his wife.
4. **Senator John Best,** (R-CT) Chairman of the Committee of Judiciary and three other committees. He was taken out at 08:47 hours by a sniper's shot as he was leaving his horse stable building on the grounds of his walking horse farm near Waterville, Connecticut.
5. **Keith Warton**, (D-PA) Secretary of Defense an Executive Cabinet Member. He was killed by a sniper's shot at 08:57 hours while driving his car on the road leading out of his farm in Ramp Hill, Pennsylvania. His car crashed into a tree.

So, what do I have to go on? Not much, just probably five professional mercenaries or military trained snipers that had a tight schedule to make their hits. Each shooting had to be part of a master plan which was executed perfectly. So, that means a lot of time was put into this project. It must have taken a leader, a plan expediter, a training area, five recruited, dedicated shooters and, above all, money! Which could spell, cartel. Then again, maybe not?

I'll just have to wait for the autopsy reports to find out more, especially the type(s) of projectiles used. Did they pass through the targeted areas or will some be found embedded in something? It will take five well trained teams to explore the assassination areas for clues. A sniper usually always leaves a clue. But, in this case, time was on their side and they may have been instructed to be sure not to leave any clues. The type of weapons used, will maybe tell me more of what I need to know.

I don't have much to go on for the four o'clock meeting. Maybe, there I'll learn a thing or two. I got a hunch they're going to stick this whole mess into my lap. If it doesn't get solved my neck is on the line, but if it does, they'll all take the lime light. So, what's new? That reminds me of a song, *"Pack-up all my cares and woes, here I go, bye, bye black bird."*

PRESIDENT'S FOUR O'CLOCK MEETING

Approaching the door I met James Thorne, the Vice-President, and Todd Gettem, the Attorney General. Once inside we were greeted by John Domel, the Director of the Federal Bureau of Investigations, General Josh White, the Chairman of the Joint Chiefs of Staff, Edwin Cage, the Head of National Security Affairs, John Holden, the Counselor to the President and his two advisors, Jane Moore and Dan Griff.

In times of a crisis, Cage always has a meeting in the Situation Room to update the President on the latest news. Cage opened the meeting by saying, "Gentlemen, you all know each other and this little get together is going to be, shall we say, 'a work shop' meeting to bring President Stone up to speed on what we think these assassinations are all about."

At that point President Stone put his two cents in with, "Gentlemen, there is no need to remind you of the grave necessity we have before us. The sudden assassinations of these five high ranking officials of the United States Government is beyond anything that has ever taken place in the history of this country.

"All we have at present is a message that stated, **'It begins, Zapata.'**
Does this message tell us what this dreadful event is all about? Mr. Gettem, give me your honest opinion and rundown on this situation as you see it. Mind you, this is no time to hold anything back."

"Mr. President, are you sure that you really want to know my honest thoughts and not just some political garble."

"Yes, Todd. I've never been surer. Please proceed."

"We all know our history and what that Mexican hero, Zapata, meant to the poor peasants of Mexico. There is no need for a history lesson, but gentlemen, are we getting a very strong warning of what is or going to take place in this country?

"This action against these five specially chosen high ranking officials must have a clue into what the next move by whomever is responsible for this morning's events. Three senators that chair certain committees and two politicians in controllable positions were put to death within one hour. Who and how many will be next?

"In the course of the last several years this country's media has revealed, to the public, the audacious and blatant disregard that we here in Washington have for the demands of the average citizens as to how we are conducting this country. The general public now realizes that we work for the rich elite, not them.

"If we look back to the presidency that brought on the very unpopular war in Iraq, lies, and, couple that with the troubled results of the Korean War, I think you can get my drift on how this country's citizens feel about the elected officials. They are not dumb. It has become very obvious, especially in the last election, of what money can do to elect officials. And, the news media's are opening up many cans full of worms pertaining to what money can buy and flows into political campaigns for elections.

"Certain laws condoning immigration, agriculture, drugs and environmental issues that we let slip by without any concern for the health and well-being of Mr. Average Citizen is so obvious a grade school child can see it.

"We here in Washington claim that the country is ruled as a Democracy and its citizens are free to vote for the people best qualified to serve them. Well, we know that's a lot of bunk! Money elects politicians, pure and simple.

"The people have realized that there is no Democracy whatsoever, except for those of the upper one or two percent of this country's population. All Washington and the states do is find ways to lie to the people and tax them so they can spend more. The Republicans cry for less government, yet every time they gain power the government gets bigger. Local governments and big businesses are getting rich off the taxpayers' backs. High cost of living and low wages are all Mr. and Mrs. John Q. Citizen get for their efforts.

"The Supreme Court (Citizens United & McCutcheon vs. FEC) has ruled twice in favor of private interest groups, such as, big powerful corporations, unions, foundations and financial institutions to use money to buy elections.

"Even our own government releases false statistics about the goings on in our nation's financial district, Wall Street. The idea of 'too big to fail' just doesn't set well with the average working person. They wonder why we let them get that big.

"It's as simple as this: We only listen to money, not the people of this country and there are hundreds, if not thousands of militant groups in this country, just waiting for a Zapata to rise up and lead them. Well, Mr. President, you asked."

"Yes, Todd, I did. And, I know the way our politicians see the Preamble is actually, **we the government**, **and not we the people**, but we can't change it back to we the people without the voter's help. One thing that we don't need in this country is a revolution. We have to nip this assassination thing in the bud, and I mean like right now! What I want to come out of this meeting is something a little more positive to our crisis at hand."

"Mr. President, I might be able to add some assumed facts to what we already know."

"Yes, I was hoping that you, Mr. Sunday, could come forward with something."

"We can assume that the assassinations were carried out by professional ex-military trained snipers or "for hire" mercenaries. They were operating individually with a carefully planned operation. A master plan had to be devised to carry out such precise killings. That tells us that there is a leader who recruited these shooters, a plan expediter, a weapons buyer, and a training area. I can assume it was a group effort which means it took a lot of money. That possibly denotes a cartel or terrorist group.

"Then again, maybe not a terrorist group. There are many disgruntled wealthy private citizens, with hidden agendas, that could possible fund this type of operation. The autopsies should give us some ballistic clues, which might lead us to a weapons' buyer.

"I have assigned five expert teams to sweep the areas of the assassinations for any clues. The shooters would have to have visited the 'kill zones' prior to the assassination dates to be able to set up positions to shoot. They or their transportation may have been seen by some one. So, the search teams must canvas each entire area for witnesses to anything that may have been noticed.

"I believe that the Director of the FBI should also select five teams to conduct a second investigation of the areas. How about it, John?"

"Well, Mr. Domel, can the FBI handle the task?"

"Yes, Mr. President, we can. But, first, I'd like to remind the Attorney General that the situation up on the Hill isn't as plain as he would like to make it. Both Houses set the pace for passing laws and bills. We may have some influence, but money talks and bullshit walks.

"The average Joe Citizen is quite comfy engaging in political talk in their living rooms, but rarely get off their butts to do anything about it. It boils down to the old clique, *'I'm just one vote, what can my vote do?'*

"In Detroit, in 1906, a famous Democrat and Socialist made a speech pertaining to the capitalistic environment this country is in and offered a solution. I can't quote it word for word, but the jest of it was in telling the nation not to follow him or anyone else, but to look to themselves to get out of their present capitalist grip.

"Gentlemen, I'm sure we all remember the beginning of the Project for the New American Century (PNAC) IN 1997. It hasn't disappeared. It only went underground and its founders and signers still lurk in the shadows of our government. The rich and powerful people who backed the known politicians of this agenda just found a new way to take control, money!

"Todd Gettem brought to light two Supreme Court ruling proving my point. We are, and I'm sure all of us realize what we have done in the Ukraine attempting to get them into NATO is to align our allies on the border of Russia. We helped to install the present Putschist's regime and this move could have put this country between the rock and the hard place with Russia.

"Russia has a strong leader and last Saturday April 5th, a Russian government spokesperson stated, 'One more step toward the Russian border can change things.' Any NATO enlargement can only compose a serious threat. If this country and NATO take aggressive military advances in helping Ukraine, Russia will have to take serious measures to ensure its own security.

"What I see being created is a walk down a path which leads to WW III. Now, to answer your request, Mr. President, of what I think these assassinations are telling us. It's a warning sign to harshly tell us here on the Hill that we better get a hell of a lot more realistic '**ACCOUNTABLITY'** in our way of electing officials and stop them from jigging and lying during campaigning.

"It's time for this government and all the world's governments or dictatorships to agree on a global order governed by **LAW not WAR.** So, in conclusion, this is what I believe is behind the assassinations. And, I'm sure within a day, we will find out the demands wanted by whomever is at war with the government. Yes, Mr. President, I believe we're at war. My department will do whatever is necessary to locate and arrest the responsible person(s).
You can be sure of that, Mr. Sunday."

"I read you loud and quite clear, Mr. Domel."

"General White, the floor is yours. Please proceed."

"Mr. President, I'm a military man and I believe that this country should be always protected at all cost. I do not believe in aggressive action against any country to gain control over them. But, the powers to be in the state capital are more interested in *Imperialism* and have embarked on a strategy to drive a rule by *Hegemony* over the Middle East and more broadly the landmass of *Eurasia.* Trillions of dollars are being spent by the richest people of our great nation to rule the world's energy sources. They want to own all that Mother Nature possesses: land, water, oil, natural gas and minerals.

"I pose a question? Does Washington want war with Russia? Because what we are doing in the Ukraine just might bring that upon this country. Russia is the main supplier of natural gas to Ukraine and other respectable countries. They have just recently stopped their discount to the Ukraine to stop our intervention in the Ukraine government. From start to finish the Ukraine crisis has been instigated by the United States' imperialism, and we all know the brothers and the other wealthy elite families and organizations behind it.

"Fabricated lies printed by certain media's have recently been retracted about the Iraq war and in Syria. Lying to the public must stop!

"If there is anyone in the room that didn't understand my meaning about this country's imperialism movement, please allow me to define *Hegemony:* It's an indirect form of government and imperial dominance in which, the **Hegemon** or leader, rules geopolitically subordinate states by the means of **power with the threat of force, rather than direct military force.**

"Last, but not least, I and my Joint Chiefs of Staff will do whatever is expected of us in this present grievous matter, Mr. President."

"General White, your views are well taken. And, I will do everything in my power to avoid a military action with Russia.

"Vice-President Thorne, you have the floor."

Before the Vice-President could utter a word a loud knock was heard and all heads turned to see Hal Reed, the White House spokesperson come barging in.

THE MESSAGE
"Pardon me Mr. President and gentlemen, but I have news from **Zapata!**"

He handed the communication to the President. The expression on the President's face changed from inquisitive to dismay and puzzlement. He stood there staring at the message, probably wondering what to say. Looking up from the message, he took a deep breath and said, "Gentlemen, I have in my hand another vicious threat and a demand. It reads:
'Tomorrow another will be assassinated to prove the seriousness in what shall

be done to change this country's ways of electing politicians and how this country is governed. The elite agenda of Oligarchy must be stopped. Mr. President, you have ten days after tomorrow's killing to call an emergency meeting of the Senate and the House of Representatives. Just prior to that meeting you will receive another communication of what changes that must become laws. Your years in the Oval Office are coming to a close. Remember: 'Yes we can! Change we need Change!' "

All were quiet. Amazement and awe filled the faces of those present. Who was next? Everyone looked to the President to speak. He turned and walked to his chair and sat down and raised his right hand and motion all to sit.

After a few moments he said, "Reed, get your staff to start calling all the members of both houses they can reach to warn them, and I mean, right now! Tom Sunday, get your ass in gear and you Mr. Domel do the same! Get those teams out there now! Find this arrogant S.O.B. We will not be intimidated.

"Cage, it's your job to inform both houses of a meeting in ten days, which will be Friday, May 16, and that's this year 2014. And, I mean, ever damn one of them that is alive to be there, wheelchairs and all! Reed, you see that those men get a copy of this demand. That'll be all gentlemen, except Mr. Reed, you remain!"

The room emptied, except for Reed and the President. The communication was in the form of a news wire from the Associated Press (AP), which was addressed to the President.
It originated from a sidewalk café in Milwaukee, Wisconsin.

Reed spoke breaking the silence, "The FBI's office in Milwaukee is already at the café. We'll have their findings within the hour, Mr. President."

"Yes, Reed, but by now the whole world knows of what is happening in this country. My private line will be busy. Be sure to explain to my secretary to be polite in telling them that I'll get back to whomever calls as soon as possible. Now, go man, I've got to think."

As I was leaving, I noticed Tom Sunday and Vice-President Thorne talking near the window. Thorne is probably telling Sunday what he didn't get a chance to relate to the President. That area is bugged with a motion sensor and will record any conversation in that vicinity. The receiver is in my office. I'm very interested to know what Thorne's views are pertaining to the matter at hand.

Once inside my office, I fast stepped it to my desk and open my bottom drawer. I saw the tape had stopped which meant the conversation was over. I buzz my assistant and related that she should get help and begin calling all the members of both houses and warn them of another assassination threat tomorrow. I hit the tape rewind button and waited.

I heard Thorne's voice saying, "Sunday, got a minute. I like to express my views. It seems everyone except me put in their two cents as to the *'why'* concerning the dreadful situation at hand."

Sunday replied, "Ok, Mr. Vice-President, go head."

After a short pause, I heard, "I don't know your true feeling about the PNAC, and I really don't want to debate the subject with you at this time. The desire for their program to extend American hegemony by force of arms across the globe has been there since day one of the election of the man we just left, and we both know that the 2000 electoral battle in Florida was illegal and outright fraudulent. The Republican Party had to win the next election by *hook or crook*.

"The Republican Party had to ensure their rise to prominence because of their small elite group of fellow imperialists. When the new president on September 20, 2001, released his **National Strategy of the United States of America,** it was an ideological match to PNAC's **'Rebuilding America's Defenses'**. In other words it was supposed to describe America's new place in the world. The men who created and nurtured the **imperial dreams** of PNAC became the men who ran the Pentagon, the Defense Department and many in the White House. When the Twin Towers came down, these men saw, at long last, their chance to turn their doctrine into a substantive policy. That door opened and they stormed right through it.

"The newly elected 2000 Vice-President was directed to meet with the big money powers for the following six months and lay the plans to create several new identities from which they could legally obtain all contracts for defense spending, thusly using shell corporation that could control and issue what had to be done or purchased by a phony bidding process. Of course, only the so called 1% could invest in these new identities which boiled down to the manufacturers of weapons and other military needs.

"Iraq was just the beginning in a pretense for more future conflicts. The defense contracts (now owned by the elite rich) dipped into the American tax revenues quite handsomely and are still sucking it dry today.

"The news media's (who are also in bed with the PNAC) are selling the wars brutal battles. It's Rome all over again, the only difference is instead of sitting in an arena, they now sit on a soft couch in their homes and cheer for blood. This is proven by the ratings jumping off the charts every time a combat scene is shown."

Sunday interrupts Thorne with, "Hold on Thorne, are you trying to tell me that these assassinations are the work of the creators of PNAC?"

Thorne followed with, "Sunday, let me put it to you in another way. It's common knowledge that a great percentage of this town hate our black president and will do anything to bring him and his policies down. The price paid to rule and dictate to the masses of the world, which is the true doctrine of PNAC, who now, in essence, controls the fate and future of America means nothing to them, because the benefits far outweigh the liabilities.

"The people verses the powerful is the oldest story known by mankind. In the history of this country, at no time have the rich and powerful wielded so much control. Who knows what methods they will use to achieve their ultimate goal?"

Sunday interrupts with, "Well, Thorne, don't count out Mr. Joe Citizen yet. The tide of **wealth and power** can be stopped, and the men who desire to rule a global world can be thwarted. It seems it might have already begun. It will end somehow. Who the victorious will be, still remains to be seen. Tomorrow will be another black day for the Hill. I do believe that whomever initiated this assassination plot will go through with this new threat.

"The man in the Oval Office is still the President of this great country and must be respected for his elected office. Our job at present is to assist him in every way possible. Now, we both better get to what we have to do." I hit the off switch and sighed.

CHAPTER THREE
ONE HOUR LATER REED'S REPORT

"Mr. President, I have the information on the Milwaukee sidewalk café. It's in a Bohemian settlement on Clarke Street. The place is a hangout for nerds and a colorful bunch of the WIFI and computer wizards. There were no security cameras inside or around the outside street areas. The internet access is free and no code is needed to log-in. The owner was interrogated and the three computers hard drives were taken for examination. The place is now under surveillance.

"My staff and others are locating and warning the members of both houses of the pending assassination threat."

"Reed, tomorrow is Tuesday the 6th. I wonder who will be next. I'm sure that everyone receiving the message will try to stay sheltered, at least that's what I hope they'll do. The news media's will be dealing out their usual doses of racism, bigotry, jingoism and homophobia.

"I'm sure the news of the Department of Energy press release this morning will also put fuel in the mouths of this administration's naysayers. They released the information about giving Poland's fracking contracts to the company that was created during the stolen eight years of the Oval Office. And you know the ones I mean.

"That release plus the one yesterday of that Dutch company getting permits to start hunting for natural gas in the Ukraine will also add a lot of negative lies across the airwaves.

"The ears of the 939 active hate groups in this country will be red hot. Most every citizen has figured out why gold for the past five years has been on the rise. The people were conned into searching their drawers for any type of gold jewelry to sell so it could eventually wind-up in the vaults of the one percent. This idea of changing the world standard from the American dollar is spreading throughout Europe and Asia.

"Hell, that'll be nothing to the many media lies that will be told to the American people when House Bill H.R. #2847 goes into effect July 1st of this year. The media that protects the right side of the aisle has already started with their propaganda about the bill devaluating money. If that's true, the rich will have to change the way they hide money to avoid taxation. The rumors will fly about people losing their savings and the dollar devaluation. What the bill actually calls for is that all foreign banks will have to provide depositors 1099 forms to this country's IRS. Hidden money, interests and transactions are costing the American taxpayers more than 80 billion dollars a year.

"There is already the scare of the U. S. dollar not being accepted in certain countries. China started the ball rolling on that situation. I just don't know what the FED's will do when Europe and Asia start clamoring for a new global currency. The only thing that might help the FED's is the huge amount of debt the United States owes to China and the rest of the world's countries.

"Once, if they do, clip our eagle's wings it will kill the goose that lays the golden eggs. No country will squeeze any money out of China unless they control the use of it. And, sure as holy hell, Russia can't support the world. You knows, maybe what's happening with this assassination crisis's will actually unscrew the crooked politicians out of their comfy money wrapped blankets. Only time will tell.

"Reed, it's getting late and we both have a long night ahead of us. We'll see what tomorrow holds."

ANOTHER ASSASSATION

Its eight a.m. May 6th, Tuesday morning at the Reed residence. He is watching TV while sipping coffee and waiting for the news. He made several glances at the phone as if he anticipated it to ring. Glancing across the table at his wife and the children, he noticed that they were all staring at him. They seem to have curious question marks in the pupils of their eyes.

As he set his cup in the saucer, a wide smile formed on his lips trying to ease the room's tension. His cup no sooner hit the saucer when his daughter said softly, "Father, is the trouble so great you can't discuss it with us?"

"Young lady, a terrible thing is supposed to happen today and I'm hoping it doesn't. If it does you'll..." I was cut off with the newscaster blurting out... *"Senator Edison O'Neil was shot by a sniper just minutes ago while leaving his C Street residences."*

"Now, my daughter you have it. I must go immediately. Please, my dear wife, see that the children get off to school all right. Don't wait supper for me. I'll probably be quite late this evening."

While waiting for my driver, I couldn't help mentally reviewing O'Neil's last month's big push for Senate Bill 2183. The Bill was passed March 3, and the President signed it April 3, 2014. It was related to H.R. 4278. Both Bills were in flavor of the Ukraine natural gas pipelines and opposed sanctions against any country, especially Russia that tried to interfere with any action against Ukraine.

O'Neil's political career is peppered with hidden campaign donations from special interest groups. He also sits on eight sub-committees which involves Defense, Energy and Environmental issues, State and Foreign Affairs, Food and Drug Administration. He has voted on all occasions to benefit an *Oligarchy* form of government. His Senate votes are always casted in favor of disrupting and undermining the *Bourgeois* democracy and democratic rights. He was a part in the "no-no" group the very day this country elected a black President. His assassination spoke loudly for people of color.

My driver wasted no time in reaching the Capital Building. Disembarking, I rushed to the Oval Office. Entering, I said, "Good morning, Mr. President."

"Good! For whom? Oh, I'm sorry for my harshness. Yes, Good morning, Mr. Reed. We have to get a statement ready for the press. Have someone call and arrange a press conference for this afternoon."

As soon as I hung up the phone after alerting my secretary to arrange the press conference, I turned to see the President staring out the window and said, "I was in touch with FBI Director Domel and Todd Gottem, the Attorney General, on the way to your office. He has also touched base with Mr. Sunday. All three are at the crime scene as we speak."

"You know, Hal, history has shown us over and over again the right paths to take to avoid disasters of one nature or another. But, we always seem to close our eyes to the problems and hope they go away.

"Prior to the Mexican Revolution in 1910, the French nobility, in 1789, that controlled France, had the same thing occur? The French Revolution lasted ten long years and the historians emphasized the cause was a class conflict from a Marxist perspective. Its central theme was the rising of the middle class joining with the lower class, urban laborers fighting together to defeat and destroy the form of government in which a few people of nobility had the power to govern. According to history's statistics only three percent of France's nobility governed the whole of France.

"I believe, and most regrettably, we are heading in a direction of some sort of revolt. That is what I understood from the first message. The control of money by this country's one percent isn't setting well in the hungry bellies of the middle and working classes. My former opponent revealed what big money in this country thinks about Mr. Joe Citizen. Presently, in America, money talks, and I'm afraid democracy is dying under its crushing power. Or perhaps, it's already dead?"

Chapter Four
FBI's Investigation Reports

Ringgg, ringgg. "Yes, Reed speaking."

"Reed, its Tom Sunday. The reports from the five investigative teams are on my desk. Is the President ready to listen to their findings?"

"Just a minute, Tom, I'll ask."

Within in a minute Reed was back on the phone. "Tom, have you reviewed them and is there anything in them we can act upon immediately?"

"Yes, I briefed them and no to your question. Shall I bring copies?"

"Hurry. The President is waiting."

It was a five minute walk from my office to the Oval Office. On the way I joined up with Todd Gettem, the Attorney General.

I knocked and Reed answered, "Come in Tom."

"Good morning, Mr. President, and the same to you, Mr. Reed. Neither one of you are going to cotton to the findings of the five investigating teams. Just remember all of these men are highly trained in this field. The group we are dealing with in these assassinations is probably the best and the shooters are probably dead by now. Even finding out their names will lead us nowhere as in the Kennedy assassination. I'll give you the short version of each assassination separately:

'Date: Monday May 5, 2014. File numbers SPCIADC 552014-P1-5:

"Number one team investigated Tennessee's Senator Howard Lange's shooting. Senator Lange lived on his estate in Howie, Maryland, and was shot by a sniper while taking his regular jog with his bodyguard. He was shot at 0837 a.m. His bodyguard wasn't shot and radioed for an ambulance.

"He lives in Prince George County with a population of just under 60,000. His house is in the middle of ten acres and surrounded by a wooded area. From the coroner's description of the head wound, the angle of the shot was determined and that area for 100 feet in width and 100 feet in depth was examined thoroughly.

"It was assumed the sniper's rifle was a Barrett M82A1 semiautomatic chambered for a .50bmg caliber shell equipped with a scope and silencer. This is British rifle made especially for sniper shooting and has a killing range of slightly over 2,800 meters (9186.35 ft.). A projectile was found embedded in a tree, ten feet from the body and a few feet above the ground, and the assumption of the type of sniper rifle was correct.

"No shell casting was found at the shooter's nest. Only a small broken branch from what could have been a sniper's perch was identified. The shooter's nest was 50 yards from the road. Vehicle tire tracks seemed to be brushed away leaving no way to find the make of the vehicle. The residents within a two mile north and south direction of the road were canvased with no results as to a car or person being seen.

"Number two team investigated Speaker of the House, Arthur Thurston's shooting. Mr. Thurston resided in Charles Town, West Virginia, and was shot by a sniper while walking to an adjacent building equipped as a work-out gymnasium at 0842 a.m. A smashed projectile was found lying on the ground next to the side of the building. It also came from a M82A1 sniper rifle.

"His five acre estate is in Jefferson County with a population of under 6,000. Using the coroner's description of the head wound, the direction of the projectile was determined and the same pattern of search was used to find the sniper's lair. No clues of any nature or witnesses were found.

"Number three team investigative Wyoming's Senator Abe Wines' shooting. Senator Wines lived in Albany County. He owns forty acres and his house is at the base of the Snowy Range Mountains, about fifteen minutes from Baramie. He was sniper shot at 0849 a.m. while horseback riding with his wife in the lower basin of the mountains. The rifle's projectile entered his head on the left side and exited through the right ear. Again, a projectile was found embedded in a tree trunk. The entire upper perimeter was searched and no clues or tracks were found. That terrain is very rocky making it almost impossible to leave tracks. Two separate possible sniper locations were checked with no results.

"Number four team investigated Connecticut Senator John Best's shooting. Senator

Best owns an eighty acre horse breeding farm for gaited horses in Bethany County. He was sniper shot as he exited his stable barn at 0847 a.m. The sniper's bullet entered his forehead and exited at the base of the skull. It was dug out of the dirt and verified to be from a M82A1 sniper rifle. A sweep of the area facing the barn revealed no clues whatsoever.

"Number five team investigated Secretary of Defense Keith Warton's shooting. Mr. Warton resided in Camphill, a borough in Cumberland County, Pennsylvania. It's about two miles southwest of Harrisburg. Mr. Warton was sniper shot while he stopped his vehicle to leave his property's gated area to turn on to the highway. The projectile entered through his driver's side window before it entered his left temple and upon exiting lodged in the divider column between the right side's two doors. The time of his demise was 0852 a.m. The road and the surrounding grounds were searched for any clues. None were found.

"So, gentlemen, what we know from our investigative teams is five projectiles from a very effective high powered M82A1 British Barrett sniper rifle with .50 bmg caliber with a range of 3,000 meters (9842.52 ft.) that has a flight time of six seconds were used to assassinate five Washington officials. The sniper rifles were issued to a shipment for Iraq and used by hired mercenaries. We have no knowledge of what happened to the rifles after the Iraq War ended. They were either left in Iraq, sold to the highest bidder or shipped back to the States to be stored. Without a single rifle and its serial number, we can't trace were it went and to who it was issued originally. In other words, we got nothing except the shooters were definitely highly trained either by our own government, a radical or a terrorist group.

"There are plenty of cyber mercenaries that advertise for hire in the covert magazines, such as, *Soldier of Fortune, The Congo and Mother Jones*. Heck, didn't the 2000 elected Vice-President create several shell corporations for the purpose of training and using mercenaries instead of our troops in Iraq?

"Do either of you have any comments or suggestions?"

"Yes, Mr. Sunday. Would you like a cup of coffee?"

"Why, yes, Mr. President, I would enjoy that."

"Mr. Reed, will you do the honors for Mr. Sunday and Mr. Gettem?"

As Reed was handing me my cup, a knock was heard. We all turned our heads in that direction.

"Enter," was the President's reply.

In walked one of Mr. Reed's assistants with papers in her hand. She stopped and waited for directions.

"Mrs. Hallas bring them to me," replied Reed.

After Reed was handed the papers, he took a few minutes to read them. Facing the President he said, "Mr. President, these are the results of the FBI's investigation of this morning assassination of the Kentucky Senator, Edison O'Neil. Shall I brief you or do you wish to read the documents?"

"Carry on, Mr. Reed."

I began reading, **"FBI File number SPFBIDC 562014-1**. Senator O'Neil (R-KY) was assassinated by a sniper at 0828 a.m. this morning as he walked from his C Street address to his waiting limousine. The shot originated from the northwest direction of D Street according to the coroner's report. The projectile entered the center of his forehead about an inch above his nose and exited out through the spinal cord. It was found smashed on the pavement. The only place high enough to be used as a sniper's perch is the seven story Capital Police Building located at 119 D Street N.E.

"Upon investigating where the shot initiated from, it was discovered that there was a power failure in the Police Capital Building at precisely 0815 a.m. and it remained off until 0842 a.m. The electrical power system is in the basement and a time activated acid bomb was used to shut down the power transformer. That type of bomb only makes a fizzing sound when detonated. The power to the back-up system was cut prior to the failure, thusly, preventing all of the security systems to function, which included the building's video cameras. It's believed that the placing of the bomb and the cutting of the back-up systems were probably done sometime the previous day.

"Unfortunately, the system doesn't lock all entrance and exit doors when it shuts down. A search of the roof revealed a L115A3 long range rifle lying on the northeast side of the roof. It's the type used by the Capital Police Department and the door to gain entrance to the roof was unlocked. In checking the time it takes to use the stairs descending from the roof to the first floor, it was found to be six minutes, twenty-two seconds.

"Interviewing the entrance desk sergeant, it was explained that the building was quite crowded, which was nothing usual, and there was a big rush to exit the building during and after the lights went back on. All exit doors have emergency spotlights. The building's cameras were still off line, so no footage was recorded for at least thirty minutes.

"Conclusion: The blackout gave the assassin twenty-seven minutes to execute his shot, conceal his rifle or take it with and exit the building. That leaves little doubt that the shooter was already in place on the roof when the building blacked out. All of the police department's sniper rifles are kept under lock and key on the sixth floor. The secured area was checked to see if one was missing or had been fired. Results: One was missing. The security lock-code was compromised. The missing rifle was the one found on the roof.

"The report is signed by John W. Domel. A copy will be on your desk this afternoon. Mr. President, I do believe we are dealing with a very well organized terrorist group that is hell bent on gutting the interior of our government by killing its elected officials."

"First of all, Mr. Reed, be sure Mr. Domel gets my compliments for an amazing detailed report in such a short period of time. And, as to your beliefs on the matter, I'd like Sunday's opinion to assist me in gathering my thoughts."

Before I could reply to the President's query another knock was heard. I checked my watch, it was 12:01 and several waiters pushing carts entered the room.

"Well, gentlemen, you'll be joining me for lunch. Mr. Sunday, I can get your opinion while we take a break for some nourishment. Mr. Gettem can follow."

Before responding to the President's request, I began to ponder what knowledge I knew about terrorist groups. Before the 2000 election, there were only a few terrorist groups in the Middle East and one or two known ones in the United States, but since that time there are now over 60 in the United States and a known amount of 165 globally. That administration stimulated a lot of global hatred.

Should I bring up the subject of Vice-President's Thorne PNAC? One of those wacky *think* tanks here in D.C. came up with the idea in 1997 and it was brought into play after the disputed election of 2000. The men that aided in electing the 2000 President made sure that he placed in his cabinet and in other high positions, creators of their dream "The **P**roject for the **N**ew **A**merican **C**entury" which is their idea of a ***global empire*** dominated by America. No, I think I'll let Thorne hang himself with that one. Besides, I think he wanted our conversation to be kept between us.

Almost fifteen years have passed since the war in Iraq which led to Afghanistan, Somalia, Syria, Libya and others. In fact, I know we have almost 500,000 troops deployed in over 150 countries around the globe.

In the eight years following the 2000 election there have been more laws passed to collect personal data on the U. S. average citizen. It's unbelievable the lengths the gentlemen to the right of the aisle have gone to control the citizens of this country. I'll try to explain to him that what I think is happening now is the *push-back* by a group of American people or possibly one group with a vision of a true **Republic.**

Suddenly, a voice penetrated my wall of thought.

"Tom, you haven't uttered a word in over ten minutes. Are you stuck on a problem?"

"Oh, no, Mr. President. Just reviewing what to say to you about this morning's assassination."

Just then the President's red phone rang. He stirred while forcing a small smile and excused himself. It was probably the ambassador to Russia, who is always the first to enter the diplomatic niceties in any situation. The situation in the Ukraine is a powder keg with a short fuse. President Vladimir Putin has lied to NATO and the U.S. about moving his 50,000 troops. A satellite picture shows they are still there. There is going to be a lot of fireworks in the days leading up to celebration of their independence. Putin is a brilliant man and he loves his *"Mother Russia"*. He must have some sort of a plan. He's not about to lose control of Russia's natural gas pipelines.

I'm sure last evening, the President spent most of it on the phone talking to everyone on his private list. And, if he had a late visitor, and that I'd bet on, I'm sure there was no family dinner.

And yesterday's news about the citizens of Missouri's outcries about healthcare must have smeared a little dirty icing on his troubled political cake. I wonder if that will carry any weight in that Republican infested house. Having a Democratic governor with Tea Party opposition sure as hell can't be any fun.

On his way back to the table, the President asked Reed to get a hold of Domel, General White and Cage. He wants them to meet us in the Situation Room in half an hour. O'boy, something or someone took a bite out of the big guy's cookie.

Oil Tanker Car Explosions

The President told Gettem to hold his thoughts till later. He stopped mid-way to the door, turned toward me and said, "Sunday, find out as much as you can before our little get together about the oil tanker cars explosions with uncontrollable fires that have been going on around the U. S. and Canada. I believe they are tied to Virginia's recent oil company's explosions and destruction of their new "safer" tanker rail cars. I want to know if all of what is happening is tied with these assassinations."

What the President probably doesn't know is the oil companies are burning off $million a day in natural gas. They build the oil infrastructure first because oil is at $95 a barrel and the amount of natural gas (1000 cubic feet) you get with it is only $4.25 cent. Which you a company invest in first? That's a no-brainer. Presently, Western North Dakota is second only to Texas in oil production.

I do believe that the exploration and fracking of the Bakken shale foundation is quite premature. But, how does one stop greed?

A plan must be made before too many days slip by. It's Wednesday the 7th, only nine days to get ready for the congressional meeting. I had just stepped through my office door when the phone rang. It was Wayne Albrite seeking any news.

"Hey, Wayne, sorry that I haven't got back to you. But, Bro, the cake is in the oven and how it will come out is going to happen within the next few hours. But, I need some input from you. The President lightly pressured me into finding out what I could about these "Bomb Trains". Can you fill me in with a quick overview?"

"Tit for tat, Bro. The quick scenario is the CDX Train that jumped the track at Lynchburg, Virginia was the last of a nine month string of derailments in the U. S. and Canada. I believe there were 15 tank cars destroyed. The fires can't be put out. They are contained and allowed to burn-out. Flames rise-up as high as two hundred feet into the air.

"The Global Partner which operates the Port of Albany has set a moratorium on the old type tank cars. The new tank cars CPC-1232 is what they want to arrive at the terminals by June First of this year. Whether the derailment are terrorist attacks is any one's guess at this point. A lot of speculation, but no concrete prove. I can dig a little deeper if you want?"

"Ok, find out what you can. I'll be in touch as soon as the President comes up with a course he wishes to take. As far as what has come of the FBI's and the CIA's teams investigations, we have no clue to whom or if these assassinations are connected to any terrorist group. All we have are six spent projectiles and the knowledge that the last sniper shooting of Senator O'Neil was from the Capital Police Building. Their security room with their sniper rifles was compromised and one was found on the roof. It was clean as a whistle. The four men with the code to the electronic locks are being interrogated.

"The building suffered a total blackout at the hand of the assassin for approximately thirty minutes. The other five assassination areas were thoroughly searched with no luck at all. These assassins are specialists, trained by a foreign government or possibly our own. My personal thoughts on the shootings. It has been in the making for several years and we having seen the worst yet. This group is hell-bent on putting their agenda in front of John Q. Public. If you're looking for a topic to what this is all about, how about 'The return of dignity to the United States political system.' Wayne, that's all I've got at present. Remember, no press. Even though, I'm sure our conversation has been taped."

"I'll mums the words. But you have given me enough to toss out in parts if necessary. Later, Tom. Oh, wait. Maybe I can give you a chuckle.

The Republican primary election ticket is beginning to give the press a comedy field day. It seems that a certain Tea Party candidate has reached the needed fifteen percent to be put on the coming Republican Primary ballot. There is a pussy fight going on between the two and now the Tea Party guy has announced he will take a $million bucks to removes his name. Boy, this party produces all kinds of idiots. Doesn't he know it's against the law to sell a seat or a vote? I thought that Illinois Governor fracas a few years back about selling a Senate seat proved that wasn't the way to go. I guess there is one born every day."

A chuckle was right. The elected or want to be elected politicians are really off in the trees somewhere. But, that's good news because the voting public should be aware of being elected has become "a racket", it's a very cushy job. According to the Federal Commission on Election Funds, they aren't supposed to keep the money to spend at will, yet they don't have to give it back. There are several ways a candidate can use the money or just keep it if they are going to run again. No one keeps track of expenses that was proven when a certain female candidate from Alaska came into focus about how she was spending her donation money. I believe a family payroll or something to that effect.

Now, it's best that I make my way to the Situation Room. In route my thoughts wander a bit. The oil tank car fires and the Ukraine gas line problem mixed into a gas and oil pot pie.

Ronald Reagan, our 40th President thought he ended the "Cold War". Bull crap, Russia
will never give up the idea of *"Mother Russia"* no matter who sits in the Russian President's chair. Russia needs money and the Ukraine spells m-on-e-y. Ever since the end of the "Cold War" the White House's powerbrokers during the eight years (2000-2008) had strived to get their dirty greasy little fingers on the oil and natural gas rights in the Soviet Union. When did the "Cold War" end? Well, that has become a matter of debate.

A lot of things happened in December of 1991. Mikhail Gorbachev stepped down and Boris Yelstin became President of the new Commonwealth of Independent States (CIS), a loose connection of old Soviet States. Now there is Putin.

Vladimir Putin is no fool and he realizes what the plan of the Project for the New American Century (PNAC) and its policy document of Rebuilding America's Defense (RAD) is about global control.

Situation Room Meeting
Arriving at the Situation Room's door, I knocked and heard, "Come in."

I was late or everyone else was early. After nodding to everyone, I sat down in my usual chair. This is one place you don't play musical chairs. I tried to surveyed their faces: Reed was looking at the President as if he wanted to say something, Domel's head was down while he was busy turning pages of his notes, General White was leaning over toward Cage whispering something in his ear, Cage was nodding his head as if he agreed with White, Thorne was eyeballing me. I suppose he was trying to figure out what I going to say. And Gettem was writing something on the cover of his file. The only vacate chair was a dead man, Keith Warton, the Secretary of Defense, a constant buddy of General White. There isn't a need any more for a human to take notes. It's all done electronically and later transcribed. We all get copies within an hour after adjournment.

I was distracted by the President's voice, "Gentlemen, I would like to start off this meeting with telling you that I've invited Mark Kelsey the Secretary of State to join us. He will fill Keith Warton's chair. He rushed back from Nigeria after he was advised of the assassinations. You all are aware of the huge female kidnapping situation there.

"His knowledge of global terrorist groups and AFRICOM, which is fighting several terrorist groups across Africa, and is one of the nine Unified Combatant Commands of the U.S. Armed Forces headquartered in Kelley Barracks, Germany. I want his views and input in addition to all of yours.

"We will get started with Tom Sunday's review of the situation at hand. Let's continue where you were going give me your take to help me assess my thoughts on what to do. After Sunday, each of you gentlemen will have his say. Begin Mr. Sunday."

"Mr. President, as I brought to your attention previously, I'm afraid we are up against a well-thought out plan. The precision of the assassinations are flawless as we have found out from our investigative teams. Absolutely, no clues. And to make us believers of their threats, they killed another Senator in our own back yard using, of above all places, the building of the Capital Police as a sniper nest. Topping that off, the sniper rifle was one belonging to the Police Department. Talk about rubbing our noses in our own dirt.

"Whomever planned and trained the men to execute these unspeakable crimes is no rank amateur. His or their knowledge goes deep into our own governmental departments. Processing the security code numbers to unlock doors in the dark and slip through undetected police building can only mean a detailed plan of the building of which is in a vault somewhere in Washington. How many men in this room know its location? Do you Mr. President? I doubt it. Our Senator's private lives are known, even the movements of everyone in this room have probably been manuscript. Meeting and agendas are readily available because there is too much loose talk during and after working hours.

"Senators, up until now thought they were Gods and could walk on water. Openly bragging about their wealth and how much *"payola"* they get from all types of sources. The whole country has gotten to know that being elected is *"a racket"*. The media's are beginning to educate John Q. Public to personal and business practices of big industries and foreign money flowing into this country to elect officials so they can get aid in goods and arms. The U.S. has become the supermarket of the world in defense weapons.

"During the WW Two, there was a slogan *loose lips can sink a ship*. Well, are loose lips getting ready to take down our government? Whatever group we're up against is telling us in no uncertain terms, *take heed America* you are losing the fight against *corporate oligarchy* and the *bourgeois* and that we are presently under a *hegemony* form of government. Since the year 2000, this country, and we all know it, has had the democracy of the United States eviscerated piece by piece.

"The rulings of the Supreme court for almost unlimited campaign donations, the removal of certain citizen's personal rights and other laws that have been passed reflect the strategy of capitalist to remove all barriers in their quest of the complete dominance of political life by the corporate and financial *oligarchy*.

"Now, I've brought out into the open what most of us wouldn't say in fear of losing one's position. But, regardless of what happens to me, I want to stop any further bloodshed. Whomever has done what is done has given us the time to cause a change in our government. This meeting on the 16th of this month has to show that we, as a country, are ready, willing and able listen to the voice of the people and not the voice of money.

"Mr. President, I hope that what I have said, and, I do believe, this is the reason behind these assassinations will assist you in convincing both houses of the serious gravity of what lies before this nation. If, in my estimation, whatever demands are asked of the houses they find a way to meet or compromise with whomever we are dealing with. Someone out there is speaking for the masses, so I believe Congress should hear the voices of the people not capitalist."

Silence laid like a heavy blanket over the room until John Domel spoke, "Mr. President, I tend to agree with most of Tom has theorized, except, we can't show a weakness either. The United States has put itself, through certain profiteering laws, in the granddaddy of all granddaddy's position throughout the globe. Our elected officials lie in campaigning because they know they can get away with it. Republicans are adamant in not changing their position on gun control, abortions, immigration laws and global warming because they are afraid of losing contributions by big business. Yes, the Supreme court's rulings in like the McCutcheon and Citizen United cases plus last year' Shelby vs Holder case, which gutted the voting rights of people of color present an open disregard for the average citizen.

"You, Mr. President, broke the colored bearer when it comes to the highest office in this nation. The voice of the people was heard. And, I personally know you have used every power at your disposal to help stop the big divide in classes. But, with all due respect, your office is limited to the powers of Congress. And, as the public views that power, they are bought and paid for by the wealthy elite. They live in a world feathered by money and perks far above the working classes. It was a great boon for the Democratic Party when your opponent used the forty-seven percent factor in his Palm Beach dinner rally. It showed at the voting poles that the people wanted someone who had them in mind to be elected into the oval office. They wanted and needed a change in government."

"Thank you Mr. Domel and you Mr. Sunday. Yes, the time did arrive to up-lift the everyday standards of the working and underprivileged classes. But, one doesn't realize the political workings of Washington until one sits in the chair of the oval office. Things aren't as cut and dry as they appear, there are tiers and levels buried in soft money beyond one's imagination. I'm sorry gentlemen, but all of that is a matter for another day.

"Well, General White have your go at it."

"Mr. President, with all due respect I disagree in part with the CIA's and FBI's assessments. I don't think we should spent time worrying about what John Q. Citizen wants and needs. We have the US Department of Health and Human Services (HHS) and the Center for Medicare and Medicaid Services (CMS). Let them worry about that. Our concerns should be in building America's defenses. We should strengthen our strategies by getting more permanent military bases in Southern Europe, Southeast Asia, Africa and the Middle East. Spend more money modernizing our U.S. forces by developing a larger global missile defense system. Cyberspace must be under our control, and, last but not least, increase our defense spending, in fact, we should double it."

"Whoa, slow down General White. All that you said is for a future debate. It's the crisis at hand that I'm concerned to bring under control. You and I can discuss your military concerns at a later date.

"Well, it's time the Attorney General, Mr. Gettem that you vent your opinion and assessment of this crisis."

"Thank you Mr. President for allowing us to speak our true thoughts. It's my belief that the American public is tired of not only being ruled by bogus bought and paid for politicians, but also using our men and women in a game of war for profit. It's the oldest and most profitable way of the wealthy to make money beyond the working men and women's imagination. It's the only way profits are gauged in lives. Out of a war the bankers, big companies and wealthy individuals acquire the rights to extracting the earth's vast riches. It seems we are always getting ready for another conflict because it pays high dividends to the already rich elite and that's who gets the money.

"We all know that it would be far cheaper for the average American to stay out of foreign governments or countries conflicts The normal net profits for a business of any size in America is in the range between six and fifteen percent, but in the case of a conflict or a war the sky is the limit. The rule of thumb is to get all that the traffic will bear. You know it is easy to tax the working class to get money for a *police action*.

"Let's look at what it takes to have a conflict with another country or even to assist another government: Uniforms, shoes, heavy weapons, gun powder, bullets, missiles, armored equipment, tanks, ships, food, oil, gasoline airplanes, plastic, wood, leather, medicine, and even medals to decorate the soldiers to name a very few. That's $billions of U.S. dollars.

"Now who pays the bills for these items? Of course, the American taxpayer. They pay before, during and after a conflict. But, the soldiers pay the biggest of the bills with their bodies or their lives. How about when they are discharged. Many have physical and psychological problems and remain depend on the services of the government to treat them. War ruins families and leave an unbelievable toll on a nation citizens.

"It's my opinion, whomever is causing our present crisis is telling this great nation to stop waging war for the profit of a few at the expense of the many. We can't be the world's police force. There can never be **_global domination_** by any country. History relates the many stories of those who have tried it.

"Well, Mr. President, now you've got my two-cents worth."

"I say, it is a great deal more than that Mr. Attorney General."

"Mr. Kelsey, this is your first visit to our crisis round table of discussions. Would you please, in as brief of a way that you can, explain your take on why those particular six government officials were singled out to be assassinated?"

"Mr. President, I will try. Senator Lange was a _devil in a military uniform_ and was always against anything to help veterans and that doesn't sit well with patriot Americans. Senator Abe Wines is Senator O'Neil's y_es boy_ and pops-up out of his suit's handkerchief pocket every time he speaks to say yea or nay. Senator O'Neil is the leader of the _no-no pack_ and openly shows distain in Congress and the media toward you Mr. President basically because you are a man of color. Killing him is like cutting off the head of a venomous snake. Speaker of the House Arthur Thurston is the Republican's _stringed puppet._ Pull his string and he will dance to any favorite Tea Party tune. His mouth spews whiskey nonsense, except when his is in tears. Senator John Best has Wall Street _money in his eyes_ interest in his every vote. The Secretary of Defense Warton seems to be a _tapping war monger_ and has openly danced to any tune of going into any conflict that will benefit the elitist. Actually, I could write a chapter in a book of anti-America Senators and government officials on each of these deceased gentlemen. That's if I was writing a book?"

"Ha, thank you for bringing a little light critique into a dreary situation. And, maybe after this crisis is over you will be able to write that book.

"Now, Mr. Sunday and Mr. Domel, I want both of you to use every resource to pick-up and interrogate all known members of any terrorist group, drug cartel and mercenaries around the country. Mr. Gettem, you be sure that these gentlemen get all the necessary legal tools they need to carry out my orders. Dig gentlemen and dig deep. We only have eight more days until the houses meet. I want to be able to counter attack in some manner should we get the opportunity. We aren't going to get a chance to second guess whomever or what group is creating this crisis. Mr. Kelsey, you get together with Domel and Sunday privately. As far as the rest of are concerned, I want each of you other gentlemen to assist Sunday and Domel in any way you can. Just don't get in their way. Any questions? And do I make myself clear?"

Simultaneously, we all said, "Yes, Mr. President."

"Then gentlemen, let's get to it. Reed, Sunday and Domel, please remain for some final instructions."

Our meeting was short and brief. Mr. President wanted Domel and myself to know that he was instruction Reed to select a crew to investigate the flow of information that's leaking. Sort of a _witch hunt_ in each White House Department. Then, he asked Domel and myself to leave while Reed remained.

Chapter Five
Reed's Private Request

"Mr. Reed, I have a private request of you. Mr. Domel was vetted when he was confirmed in July of 2013. I know he is a staunch Republican and is very conservative in his views. But, I'm unfamiliar with several facets of Tom Sunday's record. My appointments of the four previous Directors, two of which were only acting, has been unsettling to me.

"Several things that have happened recently seem to bother me: The meeting here of the new Prime Minister of the Ukraine and his right-wing fascist leader with the Republican Senator from Arizona and the US Assistant Secretary of State just a few months before all the trouble began in the Ukraine. And, Sunday's mid-April visit to Kiev which resulted in his refusing to call the USSAR an enemy instead of a major power. Since then the Moscow-Washington relations have soured by the Ukraine crisis.

"I know where the Arizona Senator's feelings are and that the Assistant Secretary had to back pedal, but I just don't want to get mixed vibes over Sunday's loyalties. So, I'm asking you to bring me his National Security Agency (NSA) file so I can review it."

"Mr. President, I'll be back in fifteen minutes."

It didn't seem like fifteen minutes had passed before I heard the knock at the oval office door. Looking at the door over the rim of my coffee cup, I said, "Come in."

In came Reed with a blue file folder in his hand. I thank him and asked him to leave while I read the file. Placing it in front of me, I stared at it for a moment. It was more than a half-inch thick. I flipped the cover open. Pausing, I remembered that Mr. Sunday served in the White House for four years as Assistant to the President for Homeland Security and Counterterrorism. During that time he helped in forming policies for responding to terrorism, cyber-attacks, natural disasters and pandemics. In his present position as Director of the CIA, he manages intelligence collection for analyzing and organizing covert-actions, counterintelligence, and liaison relationships with foreign intelligence services.

Typed across the front of the file was this statement:

NOTE: This file is a brief summary of the service career of the Director of the CIA.

January 3, 2013,

NSA File # 1-3-2013-A
Name: Thomas John Sunday   Born: May 9, 1971   Place: Jackson, Wyoming
Mother: unknown   Father: unknown

Comment: Left on the door step of the St. John's Chapel   Age: Approximately one week

Adopted Parents: Thomas and Edith (Nee Rice) Sunday

Schooling: Grades One through Twelve:
Colter Elementary (1977-1985) Jackson High School (1985-1989) Casper Jr. College (1989-1991)

Married: Lynn Johnson   Date: June 9, 1991

Comment: Wife died in child birth

Military Service: Fort Bragg   Enlisted: December 31, 1991
Schooling: College in Officer's Training / Officer's Candidate School (OCS)
Graduate: Second Lieutenant & (May 1992)

Military Service: <u>Delta Force</u>
    Operation Southern Watch (August 1992)
    Operation Vigilant Warrior (October 1994)
    Operation Desert Fox (December 1998)
    Operation Desert Badger (May 2004)

Military Service: <u>Afghanistan</u>
    Operation Enduring Freedom (October 2001)
    Operation Crescent Wind (November 2001)

Military Service: <u>75th Ranger Regiment—3rd Ranger Battalion</u>
    Operation Rhino
    Operation Anaconda
    Operation Harpoon
    Operation Jacana
   Operation Condor
   All Operations conducted in 2002

Comment: <u>Honorably Discharged: November 2004.</u>

Commendations: <u>Awards, Badgers, Decorations, Medals and Tabs:</u>

    Afghanistan Campaign Medal
    Global War on Terrorism Expeditionary Medal
    Victory Medal
    Medal of Honor
    Global War on Terrorism Service Medal
Defense Distinguished Service Medal
    Distinguished Service Medal
    Silver Star
    Legion of Merit
    Bronze Star Medal
    Purple Heart (3)
    Army Valorous Unit Medal
    Good Conduct Medal
    Special OPS Medal
    Silver Medal M-14 Marksmanship
    Meritorious Service Medal (3 Oak Leaf Clusters)
    Commendation Medal (3 Silver Oak Leaf Clusters)
    Combat Infantryman Badge (2nd Award)
    Expert Infantryman Rifle Badge
    Special Forces and Ranger Tabs

Government Service:

<u>White House Assistant to President for Homeland Security and Counterterrorism (2004-2008)</u>
<u>CIA – Assignment as Chief of Station in the Middle East (Saudi Arabia). Deputy Executive Director. Established National Counterterrorism Center and served as Center's Interim Director (2008-2013).</u>

Appointment: <u>CIA Director: March 8, 2013.</u>

Comment:<u> Strategist, keen observance, strong leadership and completer</u>
	Hum, the rest of the file is filled with letters of honor and recommendations, photographs, testimonies from Generals and other high ranking government officials. A very impressive file of a man who loves his country. I believe he dedicated his entire life in the service his country after the death of his wife. He has the makings of a great realistic die in the wool politician.

	I dialed Reed's office before leaving and instructed him to set-up appoints with the other committee heads for tomorrow morning beginning at nine sharp in the Situation Room. I want my Watch Teams to bring me up to speed on what I've missed in the past few days. It's best that I'm brought up-to-date on a dozen other situations. I can't let slip by me what is happening around the world. There goes my phone again.

	"Yes, Good afternoon Ambassador Riccardo. How are things going in Ankara, Turkey?"

	"At this point, quite well Mr. President. It has been over a year since the Prime Minister handed out his phony answers to the bribery corruption scandal. The trouble with Egypt seems to be mending. Although, Cairo's relationship with Russia is growing. Especially with this Ukraine problem.

	"But, the reason I've called is I need to be able to smooth over some quarrelsome talk about this coal mine collapse in Soma. To bring you up to speed about Soma, it's a town and District of Manisa Province in the Aegean region of Turkey with a populations of well over 100,000. The death toll stands at 282 and it's estimated another 300 are still trapped.

	"Yesterday's CNN news cast pictured an aide to the Prime Minister kicking a mourner at the mine site. This angered citizens here in Ankara and it triggered a riot.

	"Naturally, I've forwarded condolences from the U. S. and offered our aid in their rescue efforts. But, it was refused along with Germany's, France, Poland, Greece, and Iran's. Israel has also offered and have cancelled their Independence Day celebration to show solidarity with Turkey.

	"Things are very volatile here. The despair and dwindling hope for survivors has got this country on the edge of a revolution. It's the same story as the US problem the rich mine owners do not want to spend money on safety measures. To them the working class are just numbers and are dispensable."

	"Mr. Ambassador, you are aware of the major problem we have here in Washington. My advice to you is thread water with all the diplomacy you can mustard up. Be as sympathetic as possible and keep me informed. I'm pressed for time, so it's good-bye for now and thank you for your call."

	I swung around in my chair and started out the window. Looking out across the lawn, my thoughts wandered to Lincoln. What would he do? I've got to think and gather as much input from others as I can to help me sort out this problem. The message referred to my use of the word *change*, which was my original campaign slogan. How am I going to sell to those embedded Congress men changing the way we elect politicians? Over the last fifty years they have created laws to feather their positions beyond the reason of the common person.

	They are so accustom to soft and hard money donations it has become a religion to them. Our government's officials today are so crooked it make the gangsters of the Roaring Twenties look like grammar school children. How can I get them to kick the donation money habit?

Since the 1960s, money has wormed its way into the fabric of the government until it's nothing more than a big dollar with that all Seeing Eye. All my calls from Senators are about their protection. Sure they are scared. Can't blamed them.

And, there is the questions of why no man of color has been assassinated? How am I supposed to answer that one? There are estimated one hundred million people of color in the US or almost twenty-eight percent. Today there are probably several thousand working in various political fields in D.C. alone. Sure, I realize since I've become President that a great many people of color have gained good paying jobs, probably more than many whites. But, that's big business reflecting their position in the marketplace. What will happen after my term in office is anyone's guess. I image a certain percentage will lose their status and positions.

So many other problems exist: Mid-term elections have the Republicans, especially Tea Party ones, up against the wall and many will not get elected or reelected. The oil rail car disasters safety regulations must be up-dated to protect people along the rail lines. Ten years ago only 10,000 oil tank car moved across the country yearly, now it's over 400,000. The oil tankers are old and so are the tracks. Several countries are on the brink of refusing to trade in American dollars, Green House gases, no legislation in Congress. China, Germany and many other countries are working on climate control. Here in this country the Republican Party absolutely refuses to admit that the globe has a problem with the warming of our planet. California fires are a big problem, especially with the population shift to that side of the country. California and Texas are the most populated states.

The rest of the continents such as, Africa and Mid-East are in drought emergencies. This is definitely in a clear and present danger of the Arctic ice melting.

On top of all of those problems this Iraq fighting between the Shi'ites, Sunnis, Kurds and the rebel army is putting pressure on me to send troops into Iraq. To make matters worse both sides of the aisle are already having their 2016 candidates on the campaign trail.

Well, it's best that I get to calling each of my key Senate supporters to put pressure on the two houses to get ready to answer whatever is going to be in forth coming message.

It's the following morning:

Thursday May 8, in the White House's Presidential Suite and the President is having breakfast with his family. The topic of discussion doesn't touch upon the current assassinations problems. The over breakfast conversation is all about Mrs. Stone's agenda and the girls studies.

Reed had prepared a detailed list of Senators that the President would personally call to try and convince them that whatever strategy his committee comes up with will hopefully be the correct path out of this current terrorist problem, if it is a terrorist group.

It took three days for several hundred reports to flow into the oval office about terrorist and the various groups around the country. None of them were a fit for the sniper assassinations. It was most baffling that no group owned-up the sniper killings. Usually at least one of the Islamic Muslim groups would step forward and claim responsibility. Iran, China and Russia had their ambassadors relate their assurance that they weren't responsible.

Monday May 12, 2014. A White House letter arrived in the early morning mail addressed to the President marked "Personal". It was open by security and due to the sensitive material of a type-written message, it was immediately forwarded to the FBI lab. Copies of the message were returned to the president Chief of Staff, Dan Steele.

He phoned the President's interrupting the family's breakfast. By 9:47 a.m. Mr. Steele was handing the message to President Stone.

The President instructed Mr. Steele to notify Mr. Reed to have him notified the Vice-President James Thorne, Director of the CIA Tom Sunday, Director of the FBI John Domel, Chief of Staff Genera; Josh White, the Attorney General Todd Gettem, Edwin Cage, the Head of the NSA, John Holden, Counselor to the President and Secretary of Defense Mark Kelsey to be in the Situation Room at 10:00 a.m.

Their arrivals were within minutes of each other. All were seated when President Stone entered the room. After the nods and "Good Morning salutations were said, the President asked Mr. Reed to read the message:

The United States Government must begin to change its corrupt election process. Both houses over the past fifty years have soft feathered their elected positions above and beyond the level of this country's forefather's original intentions. We are no longer a nation ruled by the people. The present procedures of being elected have become a "racket" for a monetary and power gain. Large donations pave the way to misdirect the American voter. The Federal Government has allowed each State to invent law to curtail the vote of the minority. The voting process has become a mockery to the American people.

The extreme drastic measures of the assassinations should have shown that there are ones whom desire change. Further violence is not needed if the current elected officials will show a definite intention of returning to a government by the people, and for the people. The Federal Government should set the process of voting, not each State.

Beware, if the following changes aren't incorporated into the procedures of the way officials are elected into office a rage of slaughter will be unleased beyond thought. The houses will have only thirty days after their meeting to begin to pass the necessary changes. Nothing must stop the meeting. Any type of prevention will result in mass murder! You have been warned.

There are five days left until both houses meet and begin to undo the wrong they have created. Listed below is a partial outline of the required changes:

A. *Terms in Office: Six years, no reelection, a salary, no pension or perks after leaving office.*
B. *The House and the Senate are arguably redundant institutions. Each state shall have only two representatives in each house of our government's bicameral system. Smaller states must have the same representation as a larger populated state.*
C. *Health & death insurance while in office, only. Retirement and health benefits will be the same as any other citizen of the United States. Mandatory retirement at age 70 years. This ruling will be for all elected and appointed positions, including all higher and lower court judges.*
D. *These changes will greatly decrease the Government's budget for its political payroll. This also includes the revamping of Legislative aides duties and the elimination of outside organizations furnishing aides.*
E. *Campaign Donations: Limited to a total of $100,000.00 per candidate. No individual or outside soft money. The money will be furnished by the government, for a candidate to be chosen by the people.*
F. *Campaigning Time: Limited to six months previous to election voting date. Any violation will terminate the candidate's bid for office.*
G. *Time in Office Benefits: Salaries to range from $150,000 to $500,000,*

H. Depending on the office held. Each elected official must be in session 180 days a year. No raises while in office. Expenses when needed only. No salaries or bonuses for committee work. A session schedule will be worked out and submitted to the people for approval.

I. Electoral College: Will be disbanded. The majority or popularity vote will elect the President of the United States. The President and the Vice-President will be elected by the direct American citizen voter.

J. Voter's Card: Each state will have a Federal registration for a voting card

K. Similar to a Driver's License. There will be no discrimination of color, creed or race. Voting age will be 18 years of age and terminate upon death or loss of citizenship. Updated state lists will be furnished to the government monthly.

L. Currency: A return to the gold and silver standard within a five year period of time. The US dollar will once more state its backing of gold and silver and not be a Federal Note.

The above changes will become the bench mark for the way America is governed. Other changes will be recommended by the way of submitted documents and approved by a majority vote of the people.

The outcome of any mayhem that will happen is the hands of those who have corrupted this great nation. It's strongly suggested not to resist in and way, shape or form. Procrastination will be rewarded by many deaths.

All was quiet for a minute until the President spoke, "Well gentlemen, there you have what we were waiting to find out. The reason of six heinous assassinations. Terrorist group? No, I believe not. A group of American citizens, and not Mr. average John Q. Citizen. Whomever is leading this rebellion against the "bought and paid for" voting process must be connected or is within our government.

"Their knowledge and position allows for acute pinpointing of the flaws within the voting system. Can anyone add to my assumption?"

"Preposterous, absolutely absurd! We can't let anyone dictate to the United States Government. Mr. President, declare Marshall Law and the military will root out these traitors." Shouted General White as he stood up.

"General White, I receive your sentiments mixed with anger. Decisions are not made with threats for revenge. We had a President and a Vice-President a few years ago that acted and lied to accomplish absolutely nothing, except killing and maiming a great many brave men. That will not happen under my watch!

"We don't know who we're dealing with, it could be another foreign power, one of our own government identities or a combination thereof. Let me quote, in part, from the May article in the Global Research by the founder of Global Political Insight, Alexander Clackson:

"China's President Xi Jinping clearly pointed a finger at the United States, he called NATO's statement, *we cannot just have security for one or a few countries while leaving the rest unsecure* outdated thinking of the Cold War. He was referring to the United State economic imperialist agenda with its Western allies. The European Union will have to make a choice whether to continue to be a puppet of Washington, thus risking the wrath of its European citizens and eventually reaching complete self-destruction, or choosing to build closer ties with China and Russia. In other words, Russia and China are standing up to the American hegemony and pushing back against the U.S. aggression that the world had witnessed over the last five decades.

"China's and the Russia's alliance will help to alter or completely stop the growth of America's and the European's military as well as their economic global influences. This could be a welcome step forward. Western dominance over the last five decades has only achieved a more insecurity and an economic system that benefits a few, and punishes the many. That's why I said we don't know who we are dealing with in the current threating assassinations crisis."

As the President finished his last word, his phone rang. It was Dan Steele's Deputy Tab Roberts advising him that a messenger was at the door with the FBI's lab results of the mailed message. After glancing at it for a few seconds, the President read the jest of it aloud:

Envelope Stamp: Flag-Forever type. Common, purchased anywhere in the U.S.

Envelope: common standard #10 with commercial flap, 24# text weight.

Message Paper: common 20# bond cotton rag paper made from non-wool fibers.

Watermark is from the American Writing Paper Company in Holyoke, Massachusetts. It's a very common stationary paper that can be purchased in any retail store across the country.

Mailed from: Kansas City, Missouri post office #238765 Zone 18.

Date Mailed: Saturday May 10, 2014. Picked-up 6:48 a.m.

Typewriter: Remington Model electric # 34651. Out of date since 1974.

"Common and untraceable gentlemen. Carefully planned and executed. Again, another clueless communication.

Mark Kelsey broke the silence of the room, "Mr. President, if I may inject my view of this crisis."

"Yes, of course, Mr. Kelsey."

"Well, maybe it's possible we have in our midst a covert Neo-Nazi organization that has hooked-up with an Islamic Muslim terrorist group that is working with the Russian KGB to cause chaos in this country? Maybe Russia, China and Iran are using the diversion of the assassinations to gain time to wage an economic war and destroy the American dollar.

"It's no different than the politicians use to confuse the voting public while they covertly slip through the Senate a bill that will help the one percent. Most of the dirty work is done without a roll-call vote by Senators. Let's face it, a bill can contain between four hundred and six hundred pages. The senators usually receive the bills the morning of when they are to vote. No one can read and completely understand a bill entirety in a few hours."

"Point well made. But, again, a speculation. Anyone else? How about feedback from any Senator? Vice-President Thorne, you've spoken to more than a three dozen Senators. What is your take from their conversations?"

"Do you want it sugar coating or unsweetened, Mr. President."

"Just put it on the line, Mr. Thorne."

"The Senators from the Southern States think what happening is the fault of the Oval Office. The color of your skin and your socialistic ideas have risen some dead Civil War beast from their graves. The conservative Republicans and Democrats figure that your foreign policies have shown a weakness which has brought together several radical groups to ruin the power and the military might the United States has over several other countries. And, most from the left side of the aisle think it's the CIA acting under your command.

"It really boils down to they are scared enough to blame God. They also still have the glimmer of hope that money is a bullet proof shield and they, that is both houses, are gathering up a document to stop your call for the meeting of May 16 to change their power and elected office terms. They claim the meeting chamber of the "Upper House" isn't bomb proof. In other words, they want you to be blamed should anything happen if they don't meet. It's a game of "Death Chess" and it's going to be your move Mr. President.

"In fact, the two Cove brothers, Jarvis and Harry, the top money donators through their various Foundations, Societies and Institutions, are holding their 2014 "kick off" fifty thousand dollar per plate rally at Jarvis's estate Wednesday the night of the 14 th, and their having a special luncheon earlier that day for a dozen or so of their best positioned Republicans Senators and a few House members. This is when they'll have presented their petition signed by the majority of Republican Senators and as many of the Democrats that will have signed it. Of course, this money rally banquet was planned eighteen months ago to get ready for the Republican candidate to run against the Democrat candidate in the 2016 election. They want an early start to build-up a giant money war chest. But, this special lunch meeting was a spur of the moment call. Well, that's all the feed-back that I got from both sides of the aisle."

"Quite frank, Mr. Thorne. I've got an inkling that your sentiments are the same as both parties' conservatives. I hope that I'm wrong.

"I've also spoke to eighteen Senators and as many in the various cabinet and committee positions. The majority are as you have said, scared for their lives. But, not holding the meeting is flirting with murder and mayhem. Yes, the murder of who knows how many?

"It's very evident that whomever we are dealing with has prepared for this war against the government's bad politicians for quite a spell. It reminds me of the 1865, Jules Verne book which was made into the 1958 movie, *From Earth to the Moon* starring Joseph Cotton and George Sanders.

"It was about power to control the planet with a tremendous explosive called "Power X". Cotton was the bad guy and Sanders was the moral good guy. The movie seem to end in a tie with both of them being stranded on the moon.

"In the present crisis, I don't think the ending will be so uneventful. Not to be retreading old news, but the American public has been very upset with the Constitution's Amendments Two and Five for quite some time. I personally have no answer as to how to correct them, except by the voting power of the American people. But, I'm sure we all realize that the elected Senators and House Representatives aren't going to unfeather their very lucrative life style after being elected. As it was said early, **being a politician is a racket.** How sad, still very true. Otto Von Bismarck, the conservative Prussian statesman once said, **'never believe anything in politics until it has been denied'.**

"Gentlemen, this country is in serious trouble, oh, I don't just mean because of these assassinations, but because of several other things that are happening right under the noses of the general population. For instants; upgrading and rebuilding the infrastructures of every State in the Union. Financing for rebuilding infrastructures such as, utilities is being out sourced to private companies. This form of privatization is being touted to investors **as *fixed income*,** but in reality is becomes a **perpetual payment** to the taxpayer.

"All this country has to do is follow China's example on how to handle the growing need to rebuild and modernize each state's infrastructures. China owns its own banks. In other words, infrastructure financing for public projects are **interest free.** And to prove it works, the only State in this country, North Dakota has their own bank for this and other financing purposes. The return on their loans has averaged between seventeen and twenty-six percent since its establishment. In fact, the state has lower its taxes twice since 2008. Thusly, giving future generations a leg-up to be financially secure or being able to accomplish the *American Dream.*

"I wish that was the only problem facing the American people coming up over the horizon. Wall-Street and elitist multibillionaires are and have been for the past decade buying-up this country's and other country's **water rights** at an alarming rate. As an example: Oregon has a criminal law against the collecting of rainwater. A man, on his own private land built three ponds to collect rainwater. He was convicted on nine accounts fined and sentenced to thirty-days in jail. But, wait a minute, a well-known billionaire actually owns more water rights than any other citizen in this country. He controls the rights over enough of the Ogallala Aquifer to drain sixty-five billion gallons a year. So, why doesn't any ordinary American citizen have the right to collect rainwater runoff on their private land?

"These so called, **Water Barons**, of which one of them belongs to the family that Declared a war with Iraq, are buying up thousands of acres of land with aquifers, lakes, water rights, water utility companies and majority shares in water engineering and technology firms all over the world. To quote Andrew Liveris, CEO of DOW Chemical Company, **Water is the oil of the 21ST Century.**

"Unfortunately, the current global water privatization frenzy is in high-gear. The excuse to privatize is that local and state governments are having budget problems. In reality, what is happening is a giant water-rights grab by Wall Street. This undercover investment program of the wealthy elite has been on the horizon for the past decade.

"Let me prove my point. Ever since that Texas Governor got elected into the Oval Office, by Florida's slight-of-hand Electoral College trick, he and his father began buying huge parcels of land in Northern Paraguay near their family's friend the Reverend Sun Myung Moon. Reverend Moon owns the Washington Post and has throughout the years been one of their biggest money benefactor by extending them millions of dollars in loans.

"Now, you say, why? Well, that's easy to answer. Paraguay sits on top of a gigantic aquifer. And, let's not forget that Paraguay was the home base of the O.D.E.S.A. (*Organisation der Ehemaligen **SS-A**ngehorigen) (English-Organization of Former SS Members)*, which was or still is the German Nazi organization that smuggled high ranking Nazi's to South America after WW II for a safe harbor. Argentina laws prohibits extradition. Strange as that may seem, it's a known fact that the ex-president's family made millions of dollars banking with Nazi Germany.

"Look, the elite rich have got money coming out of their ears from owning and profiteering most of Mother Earth's resources, such as, land, timber, oil, gas, minerals, food products and now water. These are the things that human and animal life need to survive. The easiest way to control the masses is to own what they need to have in their everyday lives. Remember, George Pullman, the creator of the 'Industrial Town'. He owned and control everything his 4,500 workers used to live in, eat and drink. By the time a worker got his or hers weekly pay check they owed more than the earned each week. There are no better words to describe what's happening than in the old country song, *John Henry*, 'you owe your soul to the company store.' That's what *hegemony* is all about.

"But, enough of these history lesson. Let's get back to an important matter of potential danger. The political gathering of the Republican fund raising special lunch meeting at the billionaire's Hampton Estate. I want to know the names on that petition to stop Senators from meeting on Wednesday the fourteenth. Director Domel, I'm sure you can handle that?"

"Already working on it. Today's the 12th of May and I should be handing it to you late this afternoon."

"Gentlemen, we'll end this little get together. I have other pressing issues around the world to attend too. Sunday, see if Mr. Domel needs any help."

Sunday nodded his head and walked over to Domel to confer. They stood and talked for a few minutes, then parted. The President turned to gaze out the window. Mr. Reed approached him and they both sat down to review other pressing matters.

The general meeting took almost two hours. Before the end of that meeting Reed had called for a fresh pot of coffee for his conference with the President. Some of their main topics were the growing problems with the water rights issues, the huge Wall Street's profits which is causing the shrinking of the working population's wages. On top of those pertinent issues the unrest between the U.S. and China/Russia could develop into a real war threat. And, of course, the Iraq internal civil war situation, which seems to be growing out of proportion. We left the Iraq Government in the hands of Maliki and the Shi'ites. The big question, does our Embassy employees need to be protected?

While the President was on a three-way European call my mind began to wander about how I was going to keep secret from the American public the possibility of a possible undertow of ill feelings between the President and the CIA Director pertaining to the troop withdrawals in Afghanistan. Little known to the average U.S. citizen is the $50 billion opium crop that is produced on the lands near the Pakistan border that connect with Afghanistan. Those two areas represent 93 percent of the world's opium trade and is overseen by the CIA. That's why the poppy fields were never destroyed during the Russian and U.S. wars with the Muslims there. Sunday has a lot of pressure on him from the drug customers throughout the world. So, the big question is will President Stone leave sufficient U.S. Military troops there under the guise of "an advisory" reason, which in reality is to protect the taking of the poppy fields?

Since the 1950s, the CIA became the major transporter of opium to the Golden Triangle (Burma, Thailand and Laos) with the CIA's private Air America planes. They flew the opium to certain areas of Southeast Asia where the opium was processed into heroin, and then transported the finished product to the Western drug customers. Stone isn't the first president to become involved with this question. There was the Oval Office guy that was elected as the 41st President and of course, the guy that sat in the same office to be the 43rd President, plus a few others before them looked the other way in drug trafficking because they were privy to benefiting from the drug trade.

Drug trafficking is the best way to get money to finance covert operations when Congress refuses to give the CIA money. The CIA has been hired as the *World's Assassinators* many times and by several different countries. This has been the hidden major reason that the U.S. Government has never made any headway against stopping the "war on drugs" in this country. Why would a farmer kill his only milk cow for meat, when he has plenty of cattle?

And, of course, President Stone's connections to the CIA go way back to 1883, when he worked, for a year, as an editor for the Business International Corporation, a known CIA business front. In fact, most of the President's family has worked for or with the CIA for many years according to a newspaper called, **The Muslim Issue Worldwide.**

Well, I had more to worry about, my cell phone began to vibrate. It was the President's press secretary, Brad James. He just got an email giving him the low down of several surveys and opinion polls conducted by a couple of internet poll takers. They show results of being in overwhelmingly in favor of the changes, but harshly condemn the murderous methods used to obtain the nation's attention.

That's just great. All I need now is a whole lot of nonsense polls. Now every damn fool on Twitter and Facebook will be conducting polls. This cockamamie crap can cause a lot of trouble. Polling started way back in 1824, by The Harrisburg Pennsylvanian newspaper during the presidential campaign between Andrew Jackson and John Quincy Adams.

I sure hope that the Gallop and Roper polls don't jump into the game. They use polls for whomever advantage they favor. A poll's results are based on the wording of the questions, and the order in which they are asked to influence the results of the poll. The only good thing that can come out of these polls is that they are behind the President to proceed with the changes.

Setting down my cell phone, I noticed that the President had finished with his call. I advised him of my call. His thoughts bore the belief that there will be plenty more opinion polls. He reflected a, wait and see, attitude. At that we began to discuss other issues.

Several hours passed before a knock was heard. It was a messenger from the FBI with the information pertaining to the lunch/meeting at the Jarvis Cove estate on the fourteenth of May. He handed me a sealed envelope and I set it down in front of the President. Stone opened it and began to study the contents. I took the time to mentally review my known facts of the Cove Brothers and their corporate empire.

Their fortune began with a substantial legacy left from their parents. The brothers built an empire of multination industries with a yearly gross of over one hundred billion dollars. Their political activities include donating campaign money to get certain political candidates elected into strategic positions to benefit their business empire. Their yearly lobby expenses could quite possible support several thousand large families.

The two brothers are committed to the **Free Market Principles** of no rules on product pricing or what Wall Street calls it, **Free Market Capitalism**. And, they aren't alone in thinking the world belongs to the rich and should be governed by them. Their business empire consists of, chemicals, ink, fibers, polymers, asphalt, sulfur, gas, water, minerals, petroleum and many other products. But, as in most ultra-rich families, a peek into their family closet will provide a shady past in how they amassed their fortunes.

The other side of the Cove Brothers coin is their donations to help create a clean image with building hospitals and other types of humanitarian organizations. But, in my opinion those are just "clean up image" tokens and tax deductions.

Finally, the President looked up and said, "This is quite a list of the opposition's party names. Most of them are strong Tea Party members. It consist of, forty Republican Senators, three Democrat Senators, two Secretaries of the State and twelve House Republican Representatives. All in all, fifty-five names of scared government officials. Well, what do you think Mr. Reed?"

"Mr. President, the South has never forgot the Civil War. You know that you're hated because they still have that sick idea of believing they should own slaves. Especially in the five deep-south states. Up until the 60's the South was a Democratic stronghold.

"Presently, this country's got twenty-nine red states and twenty-one blue states, the elephants out number us. In my opinion the red states are controlled by the one percent (the money group). These Republican States have successfully block voting rights of the minority classes (blacks, Hispanic and senior citizens). They don't want women to have any rights, so they are against abortion and every other damn thing when it comes to the working class in this country.

"Republicans have grown to hate this country as much as they hate you. Some journalist have spoken out against the Republicans, Teabaggers, Anti-government supremacists and their conservative Christian base by saying they have waged an all-out war against women, minorities, middle class American, senior citizens, gays, children and even their own government. It's all about hating America because it won't submit to their irrational beliefs.

"Hell, the recent Las Vegas shooting of two police officers and a bystander proves the point of the NRA in telling these unbalance gun totin' idiots that it's alright to have automatic weapons. I frankly don't know what could stop the Congressmen from not showing up to meet the demands of whomever is out there that's trying to undo the ugly bad things that have been forced on the people of this country. I personally feel there is a definite need to change the election laws. As far as the currency reverting back to gold and silver backing. Well, President Woodrow Wilson knew he had chained and bound all future Americans to the dual horrors of the FED and the IRS. After he signed the Federal Reserve Act in 1913, he even went on record to say he had made a mistake by signing into law a monetary system to be controlled by the elitist. In fact his famous quote was, '*I am a most unhappy man. I have unwittingly ruined my country. A great industrial nation is controlled by its system of credit...all our activities are in the hands of a few men. We have come to be one of the worst ruled, one of the worst completely controlled and dominated Governments in the civilized world, no longer a government by free opinion, no longer a government by conviction and the vote of the majority, but a government by the opinion and duress of a small group of dominant men.*'

"This present crisis has even reach the Bilderberg Group. Their 62nd Bilderberg meeting is being held at the end of this month in Denmark. And, according to their original website they were founded in 1954, and hold an annual conference designed to foster dialogue between Europe and North America. Every year, between 120-150 political leaders and experts from industry, finance, academia and the media are invited to take part in the conference. About two-thirds of the participants come from Europe and the rest from North America; one third from politics and government and the rest from other fields. The conference is a forum for informal discussions about megatrends and major issues facing the world. And, of course what is happening here in America is a worldwide government and monetary issue.

"The meetings are held under the Chatham House Rule, which states that participants are free to use the information received, but neither the identity nor the affiliation of the speaker(s) nor of any other participant may be revealed. Thanks to the private nature of the conference, the participants are not bound by the conventions of their office or by pre-agreed positions. As such, they can take time to listen, reflect and gather insights. There is no detailed agenda, no resolutions are proposed, no votes are taken, and no policy statements are issued.

"I'm quite sure the recent assassinations and their effect on the world will be their main speaker's topic. Well, Mr. President you asked what I thought and there you have it."

The President was standing with his back to me looking out the window when I finished. It took several minutes before he turned around and looked into my eyes. He put his hand up and pointed to the flag and said, "Two hundred and thirty-eight years and we still having learned to respect one another. The signers of the Constitution have got to be rolling over in their graves at the turmoil facing us.

"Someone or some group is giving this country a second chance. We, the politicians of this country, have strayed so far of the course of freedom and equal rights of this world's citizens that I'm surprised the Almighty has let this planet self-destruct or struck it with a giant meteor to allow it to being all over again. Reed, we must keep trying to convince the hard-headed nincompoops of this Congress to meet and at least discuss the possibilities of the demands.

We've got only a little over three days to exert every effort to bring this meeting on the 16th to order. Contact Sunday, Domel, General White, Kelsey and Thorne to call every name on that list and urge them to hold the meeting. I'll get to work on the money supporters for the Republican Party. We must prevail in our efforts."

I left the office in deep thought wondering how much can the President take on his domestic and foreign plate. There are the problems in the investigation with the FBI's 150 shootings in criminal cases for the last twenty years that have not been explained, except to take "no action" in each and every case. All the shooting couldn't have been justified? It's the same with the immigration's border patrols shootings with their 28 shootings along the Mexican border. Sure many have been shoot-outs related to drug trafficking, but still there is no records on file about them because there isn't a bureau to accept the complaints. None was ever formed. Thusly, leaving them to do what they want at will.

The defeat of the Republican House Majority Leader from Virginia that is in charge of the force against the "gang of eight" attempt to push through their CIR bill to reform the immigration laws just got trounced by a "Tea party brat. This I believe was due to the knowledge of American citizens that the Republican Party has rigged the entire political system against the working classes.

And, of course the use of his "police action" deployment of American troops in Central and East Africa, Libya, Yemen and Uganda to protect American citizen living in those countries, terrorist attacks on our embassies, plus the aid to hunt down Joseph Kony, the war lord of the Lord's Resistance Army (LRA) and to assist in finding the 300 kidnapped young girls from the town of Chad in Nigeria. All seem to be very justified reasons for sending small amounts of troops to aid the people of these god-for-saken-places. But, the public don't think so.

We all spent the last days trying to convince the Senators to meet and begin some kind of dialogue to ward off any further assassinations. All efforts went awry. Hope, was all that was left. The hope whomever it was causing this crisis was bluffing about the rage of slaughter beyond imagination.

It was finally the morning of the 14th and as usual, the President had breakfast with his family. It was a little after nine when my phone rang. "Good morning Mr. President. I'm not going to ask if you slept well, because I can assume we both didn't. How do you wish to begin this day?"

"On pins and needles, Mr. Reed. Did Sunday or Domel get a chance to plant eyes and ears at both the luncheon and the banquet this evening?"

"I'm afraid not. Jarvis Cove's special security force is one of the best in the country. It's Academi, Eric Prince's old Blackwater Worldwide. B W was sold to a group of investors in 2010. Although, the CIA uses them on an on-going contract with our government. Nothing stay a secret very long amongst those boys. I'll sure we'll get some insight within this day. I'll keep you informed as the day progresses. For now, I suggest you go to the gym and try to work off the morning stress."

It was about twelve thirty and I was taking a sip of coffee to wash down the last bite of a ham on rye when my office phone rang. It was Tom Sunday.

His first words were, **"They're all dead,** the whole damn group. They were warned about what would occur if they did meet to discuss not passing the demands."

I interrupted him, "What group? Who's dead?

"Cove's special luncheon guests and I guess Cove's big gala dinner soiree tonight will be cancelled. There are hundreds of people already hanging around the entrances of the walled-up complex."

I gasped and said, "Am I dreaming, did you say all of Cove's special luncheon guests are dead? How? When? How did you get the news?"

"Yes, Reed. We were warned and those damn fool politicians didn't listen. I received a call from the chief of police in Wichita, Kansas. We were in the Special Forces together and have kept in touch. He told me that Mrs. Cove's helicopter pilot call him about a half-hour ago relating what they discovered upon returning from Cove's wife shopping trip.

"I've talked to Domel before I called you. We each have a team in the air, as we speak, on their way to the scene. The chief has the mansion locked down. No one but his people and ours gets in or out. There is no use wasting time now speculating on the how and the names of the victims. Let's wait until we get the facts from the teams. Domel and I are taking a CIA G650 jet and we will be on the site in Kansas in less than two hours. Advise the President before he see it on TV, and inform the President we'll contact you when aboard our return flight. We'll report directly to him after we land. In the meantime the FBI and the CIA teams will be gathering all the pictures and facts. Agreed?"

"Yes, till later." I hung up the phone and took a deep breath, opened my left hand bottom drawer and withdrew a bottle of Khortytsa (Ukraine vodka) out of it and sweeten my coffee. I held the cup to my lips for a moment before swallowing the contents. After it settled in my stomach, I reach for the phone and dialed.

"Good....No not this morning are you alone and sitting down Mr. President?"

"Yes, what is it Mr. Reed?"

"The Cove luncheon meeting is over and all who attended are dead!"

There was no response, just silence for few seconds then he said, "Do we know who and how? Have you talked to Sunday?"

"Yes. In fact, he called me with the news minutes ago. He and Mr. Domel have their Kansas teams already there. The entire estate is cordon off so the news media can't get in. Sunday and Domel are on their way by one of the CIA's new G650 jets to Cove's Kansas estate. They should arrive there between two-thirty and three o'clock. I'm to advise you that they will contact me and meet with you immediately after their return to Washington. Also, tell me if you want any others of your staff at that meeting."

"Reed, I'll be in my office in ten minutes meet me we'll discuss the detail then."

"As you wish Mr. President. I hung up and took another swig from the bottle. Gathered what I needed and left for the oval office.

I knocked and entered. He was standing in front of the window staring out over the back lawn. Without turning around he said, "It happened! The worst has actually came true. I'm appalled, sad, mad and scared. Reed, what is the news media going to do with this ghastly massacre. It's my watch and I'm going to have to calm the nation. Better make arrangements for a televised broadcast for the day before the Houses meet. I want to give the address in the upper house's chambers before Congress has their roll call. That should give us enough time to sort out the facts and have some kind of positive response to the American public of what we're going to do about this insane crisis.

"I want you and all the committees, counsels and departments under your control to help you make sure that every one that's still alive is there. That means all living Senators, and whomever are the top ranking House Representatives. Limited the House members to whomever is in control, no blabbermouths. That's if you can sort them out. Put your list together after we find out who is still alive. And tell them there will hell to pay for whoever doesn't show up.

"Tell my Chief of Staff that I'll only except calls from Russia, China, Germany, England and the Middle-East. Any other callers, just have him make up excuses to them. See to that right away, before my private line starts ringing. Leave me and return in an hour. Wait, locate a cell phone that isn't bugged, contact Tom Sunday give him the number and have him call me from the site on it. It's almost one o'clock, he and Domel should be there in another two hours. I want his first thoughts and gut feelings recorded. I also want you present to hear what he has to say. That knowledge will give us a head start in preparing for our meeting. It will also give us some time to prepare what you are going to say to the press. Have my Chief of Staff, the Deputy chiefs of Staff, my Counselor and Senior Advisors waiting outside the Situation Room. We'll reveal our plans after speaking to Sunday and Domel and will make a decision of what is to be done.

It was twenty-minutes passed two about ten minutes before it was the time to return to the oval office, when I got an email from a staffer friend of mine on the Washington Examiner, it read, **Arrogance Begets Death...It was signed Zapata.** No soon had I finished reading the email my phone rang.

"Hal, did you get my email? That message was found on the newspaper's entrance floor less than ten minutes ago. And before you ask, no we don't have any surveillance cameras in that area and no I couldn't get my hands on the original message. Gotta go, before I get heard."

I was stunned. It is going to run a chill up the President's spine. And maybe set his heart beating to a Dixieland tune. Oh, my God! Were my immediate thoughts. I printed the email, and reached for that bottle of Khortytsa. It was another ten minutes before I headed for the oval office.

I knocked and entered. He was on the phone with his chair turned to face the window. Swiveling around, he noticed the paper in my hand. He raised his hand in the motion to stop me from walking over to him. A few second later he said, "Yes, I will" and hung-up.

With my eyes locked with his as I slowly walked toward his desk. He extended his hand and without saying a word, I handed the email to him. He closed his eyes for a moment before beginning to read the email. I took a deep breath and waited for his re-action.

Looking up from the paper he said, "How can whomever is committing these dastardly deeds deliver these message from the various places? They seem to pop-up from all over. The **first** one was received by the **Associated Press** Monday May 5th, stating *It begins, Zapata*, the **second** one was on the same day from a **Milwaukee sidewalk** café warning us of another assassination, the **third** was a letter to the **White House** on Monday May 12th with demands and now the **fourth** today, Wednesday May 14th a message warning against the Senator's petition found on the entrance floor of the **Washington Examiner** newspaper only a few hours after a mass assassination. How do they do it? Neither the FBI nor the CIA has been able to trace any one of them to the sender."

"Mr. President, all of what has taken place and transpired seems to have been quite carefully planned. It certainly wasn't or hasn't been done on the spur of the moment. It seems every situation has been anticipated and the reactions of notes or whatever precisely planned in advance.

"Well, whatever, Sunday will be calling shortly. I had no sooner finished my sentence and the un-tapped cell phone rang. We both stared at it for a moment. The president picked it up and put it in the sparker hook-up. He then said,
"Yes, Sunday. What can you tell me?"

"Mr. President, may I ask you if you are alone?"

"Why no. Mr. Reed is with me. Why?"

"That's fine. I'm glad Reed is with you. The why, you will find out after I unfold the details and assessment of what I'm about to tell you. I'm sure Reed has pull this call on the speaker/recorder system. Has he brought-up the estate on your office's satellite viewer?"

"Yes, we are looking at it as we speak."

"Great. As you can see it's a very large estate and consist of a section of 640 acres of land or a mile by a mile. It's completely walled in with only a half-dozen well-guarded entrances and exits position around the property. We landed at the small Westport Airport and took a helicopter to the estate so as not to draw any attention to our arrival and to keep the press out of the loop.

"From the overhead view the estate's house is in the center of a wrap-around 36-hole golf course. Like in the center of a giant horseshoe. You can see our copter on the pad to the right of the main house. Scattered around the estate are many buildings which are used for guest houses, maintenance, horse stables, land care-equipment and various other uses. On the grounds are also tennis courts, swimming pool, a sheet-shooting facilities, a spring feed fishing lake, a small zoo, and a polo field to mention the main amenities.

"The three story building off to the right of the main house is the servant's quarters and the building off to the left is actually the utility building that houses the refrigeration, heating and water purifying system and the offices for security and property surveillance. The main house has three sections. The section on the left is a tall one story used for entertainment purposes, which consists of a banquet room with a full gourmet kitchen, a dining room with the capacity for 300 people and a grand ballroom. It also has a smaller section for informal meetings and smaller banquet affairs which is where the lunch meeting was held. These rooms are divided by a main entrance hall for greeting guest.

"The section on the right has three floors consisting of twenty-five furnished guest suites. The middle has three floors used strictly for the family and consist of a library, dining room, a dozen bedroom suites, kitchen, drawing room, a game room with a bar and movie screen, an atrium with an indoor swimming pool and a few more personal amenities. According to the blue prints the main house has fifty bathrooms and is 75,000 sq. ft.

"Each of the main house's sections are individual control for a constant atmosphere of cooling and heating. It's all in the building to the left near the entertainment section. The equipment is automatically controlled by computers and is inspected every hour by a security person. There are no maintain men, just machines in that building.

"Are you understanding my detailed description, Mr. President?"

"Yes, quite perfectly Mr. Sunday. I'm in awed at the immensity of the estate. It's more like a private town than a single place to live."

"The Chief of police related to me in flight that its estimated value on the Wichita tax roll is over one billion dollars. Of course, it isn't taxed at the estimated figure. Say, I wonder what the White House is estimated to be worth? Just kidding, Mr. President.

"That really is a not a lot of money considering their combined business empire generates well over one hundred and fifty billion dollars yearly. Their profit or bottom line is more than it takes to run the State of California, Texas and D.C.

"Sorry to have gotten off track. First, I found out that the fund raising dinner banquet that was to be held in the evening was set-up for the guest two days prior. This was done to keep the servants away from this private luncheon. Mr. Cove had sent his wife and her chauffeur-bodyguard on a shopping trip to get her out of any socializing with the lunch guest. Now, as to who was here and is dead. Mr. Domel is in the process of collecting that data and will forward it via his cell phone to Mr. Reeds' when each and every body has been correctly identified. He wanted to be absolutely sure before revealing their names. The number of dead is seventeen and consisted of Jarvis Cove, six Senators, three of your Cabinet members, the House Budget Leader, two lobbyist and four servants. That will take care of the number of the deceased. The how is a little more complicated.

"The building's atmospheric controlled computer system is the way the massacre was able to take place. As I explained earlier, each section of the main house has its own water supply and controlled atmosphere. Their death vehicle was delivered through those systems. They were all dead in a matter of a few minutes by a gas chemical warfare agent classified as a nerve agent. Or better known as sarin or GB. For that nerve agent to have a maximum lethality, it must be aerosolized into a fine gas. This makes it quite easily absorbed through the lining of the lungs. This type of nerve agent kills by blocking the body's enzyme called **acetylcholinesterase**, which in return makes the body's nerve cell to *fire* causing muscles-including the heart to have spasms. It also cause convulsions and muscle twitching tossing the person to the ground. In effect, this nerve agent prevents the proper operation of that enzyme that acts as the bodies **off switch** for glands and muscles. Without an **off switch**, the glands and muscles are constantly being stimulated causing the lung muscle to not function and prevents a person from breathing. When this nerve agent is heated to a very high temperature it turns into a gas. This nerve agent is eight times more deadly than **VX** or **soman** which are two other man-made deadly nerve agents. It's going to be difficult to find out the source of obtaining this nerve agent.

"It's similar to any pesticide in the **organophosphate** insect killing family, but much more potent. Its properties are being clear, odorless, and tasteless. It was originally developed in the Germany in 1938 as a supposed insecticide.

"It's believed to be one of the nerve agents used during the Iran-Iraq War in the 1980s. In 1997, the United States and other countries agreed at the United Nations International Chemical Weapons Convention treaty to destroy their stockpile of aging chemical weapons. By 2013,190 countries, which represents over 98% of the world's population, ratified the agreement. There were only six holdouts; Angola, North Korea, Egypt, South Sudan, Burma and Israel. The last two, respectively, have signed the treaty but have not ratified it to date.

"In 1995, the Aum Shinrikyo Cult used it to kill a dozen people on the Tokyo Metro. In the case at hand it was exposed into the air via the air-conditioning system and water system contaminating the building's air, water and food. It's heavier the air and sinks to adheres its self to anything including clothing. Being odorless it went under detected for quite some time. The amount of the nerve agent used was enormous. It didn't take long before they were dropping like flies in a heavily sprayed room.

"We inspected the computer controlled atmosphere building and found a unit attached to the supply systems resembling a normal looking computer cabinet. It was delivered there as a trumped-up replacement unit for one of the control units. According to security it was delivered Monday May 12th and was set in place by two of the company's uniformed workmen. Inside, it had the gas cylinders and a timer to release the sarin gas at the precise time of the lunch meeting. The names of the signed work sheet are probably bogus, but we have their faces on a video surveillance tape and has been checked out.

"The video surveillance tapes show the men and in my opinion they appear to be wearing facial disguises. The entire place will be powdered for fingerprints. It's my guess the only prints that will be found will be those of the security employees, but who knows? This way the team can eliminate the security guards and anyone else that's works for the estate. The delivery vehicle had the proper logo and name of the computer company. The chief checked to see if the company had one stolen. Answer, no. So, it had to be another truck made to look like an original delivery truck. I'm sure by now it has been taken apart and the pieces dumped in who knows how many places. As far as the security personnel and the employees of the estate, all will go through a complete vetting by Domel's people.

"As far as the nerve agent's delivery devise, it has already been removed and taken to where it will be dismantled and checked for any finger prints or clues to its construction or purchase. That will take considerable time. As far as the delivery and set-up team, they are probably dead and disposed of by now.

"Mr. President, it's getting late and we still have to confer with our teams. Can you or Mr. Reed think of anything else you would like to know at this time?"

"No. I'll probably have more questions tomorrow. Call Reed when you can come to the Oval office in the wee hours tomorrow. Our conversation has been recorded, so we'll be able to review it.

President Stone looked at me and lowered his head before he asked, "Care to make any comments Mr. Reed?"

I watched him walk over to his chair and sit down before I answered, "I also like to re-hear the tape before expressing any views Mr. President. But, right now, I wish to leave and get my staff working on your speech. If you don't mind sir."

He didn't say a word just waved his hand good-bye. I closed the door softly upon leaving and stood in its entrance for a few seconds. My hesitation was to ponder my next move. The decision was to instruct my staff to begin writing the President's speech addressing the nation about the current assassination crisis. Then, do some research reading on nerve agents. I'll need to give a copy to President because the look on his face when Sunday mentioned the nerve agent's name, *sarin*, showed me that he was unfamiliar with its properties.

Back in my office, I settled in to prepare for the work ahead. I drifted off in thought for a moment and the words of an earlier statesman, of which I can't recall his name, popped into my head, *"It does not require a majority to prevail, but rather an irate, tireless minority keen to set brush fires in people's minds."*

Its best that I contact the President's Press Secretary Brad James to have the White House Press Secretary, Joseph Earn and Earl Shantz, the Deputy Press Secretary, contact the newspaper reporters. Most people don't realize that the Press Briefing Room has a limited seating of 49 and the newspaper reporters have assigned seating. They are organized by the White House Correspondents Association, not by the White House Press Staff. The location has been remodel many times by several presidents. Its main location is in the West Wing and is 5,525 square feet, and is controlled by the National Security Council.

The President hasn't met with his Watch Teams in the Situation Room for the past two days. Each day three Duty Officers, a communication assistant and five Watch Teams monitor and analyze domestic and global events. Each team has approximately 30 personal from various agencies in the intelligence community and military. Everyone seems eager to pull what has to be done, together.

THE PRESIDENT ADDRESSES THE NATION:

The huge Press room was buzzing with loud chatter. People were walking about and then, the sound of the gavel! Shushes became all one could hear and then pure silence. The President was announced entering the room. He slowly walked to the podium. He set down his written speech and took hold of the podium with both hands before raising his head. Every radio and television station in the world would be carrying the President's message:

"Mr. Speaker, Mr. Vice President, Members of Congress, Members of the House, the Press, my fellow Americans and the citizens of the world:

"Before I begin, I wish to relate that there will be no questions after I have spoken, because you have been given copies of this speech. The people of this great country will have to answer the demands. It will be your responsibility to decide your own faith, as it should have been in the past.

"A great task lies ahead in the shadows of the darkness of death. Twenty-three people have been assassinated in what some group believes is to purge and purify our nation's election system. It's no secret that the people who control your lives and our government have set themselves apart and above the average working class and the poor. Their sole purpose is to bow to the rich elite for financial contributions to win elections.

"The determination of the American voter has been called upon to rectify a wrong that has been progressing for decades. Our Constitution, according to Congress today, is no longer, *WE THE PEOPLE, INSTEAD IT HAS BECOME, WE THE GOVERNMENT AND YOU THE PEOPLE!* And, that is wrong! With today's technologies of communications it may not be necessary that the House and Congress make the laws. Maybe the time has come for them to pass the laws that the people have voted upon and not for the representatives of this government's own personal agendas.

"**Greed and Power** has taken president over the need of this nation's people. Abortion, the fight against drugs and immigration are subjects of political illusions and are banned about to be used for only chaotic ruses. Political campaigning agendas are all your elected officials seem to care about. I'm a man of color and because of that color many believe that I don't deserve to sit in the Oval Office. The meaning of *ALL MEN ARE CREATED EQUAL*--- HAS NO MEANING TODAY! Why can't a woman, a Hispanic, an Asian or any other righteous citizen of this great county be elected to the highest office of this nation? A woman in the State of Florida proved that the Electoral College is inadequate in selecting the person with the most votes. Trickery and selective votes can reverse an election.

"War and global economy is being discussed behind closed doors by bankers and corrupt politicians with little concern for the rights of the general public.

"In 2008, my first bid for the Oval Office the people ask me if I could make a difference. They asked me for a change in the way they were governed and treated. On my very first day a certain group of members of our government met and organized the party of **"NO" with the intention of stopping anything that I would do for the good of the working classes and the poor. I was to be a one term President. Well, you proved them wrong. And, now is the time make the biggest changes in the history of this nation.**

"Mid-way through my second term, **Congress has don't nothing to help the citizens of this country. They even hate what is proven to be successful,** *STONECARE!* In 2006, the Governor of Massachusetts passed an Affordable Health Care Act which is still in effect and was a model for **Stonecare** due to it widely recognized success and popularity. Now, it is not a good program only because they didn't initiate it for the Nation.

"Enough said about my cares and woes. The papers have related to the American people the demands of this group that is assassinating our elected officials. Reform, yes reform is what it's going to take to stop this murdering vengeance. I'll now outline their reform demands:

TERMS IN OFFICE: All elected officials shall serve only six years in office, no reelection, a salary, no pension or perks after leaving office.

HOUSE OF REPRESENTATIVES: The House and the Senate are arguably redundant institutions. Each State shall have only two representatives in our government's bicameral system. Smaller States must have the same representation as a larger State. Namely, 100 Senators and 100 Representatives.

HEALTH and DEATH BENEFITS: While in office or retirement the Health benefits will be the same as any other citizen of the United States. Mandatory retirement of government employees at age 70 years. This ruling will be for all elected and appointed positions, including all higher and lower court judges. No lifetime jobs.

BUDGET REDUCTIONS: These changes will decrease the government's political payroll. This also includes the revamping of Legislative aides duties and the elimination of outside organizations furnishing aides to advise the newly elected.

CAMPAIGN DONATIONS: Limited to a total of $100,000 per candidate. No individual or outside soft money. This money will be furnished by the government for a candidate to be chosen by the people. No free TV ads.

CAMPIGNING TIME: Limited to six months previous to election voting date. Any violation will terminate the candidate's bid for office.

TIME IN OFFICE SALARY BENEFITS: Salaries to range from $150,000 to $500,000, depending on the office held. Each elected official must be in session no less than 180 days a year. No raise while in office. Expenses when needed only. No salaries or bonuses for committee work. A session of both House's schedule will be worked out and submitted to the people for approval. Voters will be explained in plain

English each law before it is voted upon.

ELECTORAL COLLEGE: Will be disbanded. The majority or popularity vote will elect the President of the United States. The President and the Vice-President will be elected by the country's legally registered voter.

VOTER'S CARD: Each State will have a Federal registration for a voting card similar to a driver's license. There will be no discrimination of color, creed or race. Voting age will be 18 years of age and terminate upon death or loss of citizenship. Updated lists will be furnished to the Federal government monthly.

CURRENCY: A return to the gold and silver standard within a five year period of time. The U. S. Dollar will once more state its backing of gold and silver and not be a Federal Note. This means the elimination of the Federal Reserve Act of 1913.

The above changes will become the benchmark for the way America is governed. Other changes will be recommended by the way of submitting documents and approved by the majority vote of the people.

The outcome of any mayhem that will happen is in the hands of those who have corrupted this great nation, the Congress. It's strongly suggested that the Houses do not to resist in any way, shape or form. Procrastination will be rewarded by many future deaths.

"Well, America, there you have it. Tomorrow is the day of reckoning. Will it be a Republic rule by the people or shall we chance the death of many.

"Newspapers must reprint the demands in simple language. You, the citizens of this country go to your telephones and call your State's Congressmen and demand that they meet and discuss these demands. Procrastination is not the answer, it will result in more assassinations. Sticking our heads in the sand will not make this problem go away.

"Congress is meeting tomorrow in a joint session and the results of their acceptance or denial will predicate continuing or stopping this slaughter of lives.

"Remember, we are not fighting a war, but are government is being attacked for carelessness in both house's treatment of their power over of the American citizens. I place the blame on the political parties of selling out the basic principals' that our founders meant to make this nation great. ***Change, yes, Change in the way we govern is what is needed! It must go back to we the people, not we the government!***

"This Nation must stop policing the world for the good of the rich elite. Bring our troops home and let them rebuild the infrastructure of this nation. We have the resources, might and strength to defend this country from any aggressors. Let the Middle East fight their wars as they have done for centuries, redo our trade laws and make them equal their imports dollars with our exports dollars, if a country wants aid let them paid this country with their country's resources. We must stop creating economies for other countries which only benefits the rich elite and brings death to our men and women of our armed forces.

"Let other countries use America as a model for their own economies and governments. Life is precious to us and most other countries deal in death as a matter of fact. Change our taxation laws so everyone, business or corporation pays their fair share of taxes. Let's get behind this nation and make it equal for all to believe in whatever religion they might choose, become successful to live a full rich healthy life and above all, live in peace. Any man, women or child, no matter of what creed, color or gender, should have the right to prosper and gain the American dream.

"Last, but not least. I will try to answer the question of why we can't and haven't apprehended these assassins. Every security agency of this nation has extensively followed each and every lead or clue that is available and to date has had no success. What is believed, it's not any terrorist group or other country has been responsible. The culprits have carefully planned this crisis and are amongst us because of the aforementioned demands. The only people that will benefit by changing the laws to meet the demands are the people of America.

"We the people of this great country may do different jobs, walk different paths, and have different views than our neighbors. But as Americans, we all share the same title: Citizens of America. The word *CITIZEN* doesn't describe a nationality, color or status. But it does describe what we collectively believe in, and that is America. I pray that we all act collectively to end this horrendous crisis. In closing, I personally believe that the above demands are only a beginning and that more will follow.

"Thank you. God bless America and its citizens for they are now the judges of their future."

The President smiled, and waved as he slowly walked toward the door to exit the room. The crowd's applaud with a standing novation as a tribute to their agreement.

By the time that I got to the oval office, Tom Sunday, John Domel, James Thorne, Todd Gettem, Edwin Cage and Josh White were all chatting amongst themselves. My entrance came with silence.

"Thank you Mr. Reed and your staff for an excellent speech. I know that I added a few unusual inserts of my own. But, I figured they had to be said.

"Well, gentlemen what is your consensus?"

The president no sooner ended his sentence when a knock was heard. At that the President said, "Forgive me gentlemen, I've forgotten to tell you that I also invited my counselor, John Holden, and my advisors, Jane Moore and Dan Griff to join us.

Everyone stood in silence staring at the person (s) they were talking with for a few seconds. You could almost hear their hearts beating. The President got up and walked to the windows which overlooks the White House back lawn.

The President snapped the pencil he held between his fingers that were coupled behind his back and turned around. I stepped forward and said, "I believe the combined opinion is to see that the Senate and the House meet as prearranged. I don't think we dare to suffer the consequences. It just might cause the American people to start a revolution."

"Point well taken, Mr. Reed. We all know what it take to make or change a law. Get in touch with the Senate and House for the proper introduction of the new bills or joint resolutions to start the process. Be sure they follow perfect protocol and get the bills numbered. There will be an early meeting of both houses tomorrow.

"Oh, by the way Mr. Sunday, do you have the list of names that were gassed at Cove's luncheon?"

"It's in the blue folder on the corner of your desk. Do you want me to inform the group of their names?"

"Yes, please do."

Sunday walked over to the desk, picked up the folder and began to call off the names:

"Jarvis Cove, Senators John Shell, Claude Ambers, Rick Glass, Nick Johnson, Ralph Burns and Lee Evans. Cabinet Members: Jack Howriz, Edwin Cortez and Natalie Towel and the head of the House Budget Committee, John Peters. Lobbyist, Fred Needs and Mike Shelzer. Four servants of color: Josh Jackson, Washington Roosevelt, Noah Wilson and Wilson Nelson. Seventeen in all and bringing a total of 23 persons assassinated."

Sunday return the folder to the corner of the desk and stepped back two paces.

Not much was said beyond that point. Everyone except myself began leaving the room. I remained for further instructions. We both just stood there in complete silence for several minutes before I spoke, "Mr. President, you realize that those demands can't be met in a single day because they deal with creating new bills and also changes to the Constitution's Amendments. With an early start several of the demands can be put into Joint Resolutions or bills and others into Amendment changes.

"I believe that Terms of Office and the Electoral College elimination can cover the ones pertaining to the election and the campaigning demands, the reduction of House Representatives for each State will take a separate changes to the Constitution. The changes to the Voter Card and Currency will take separate bills or joint resolutions."

"I agree, Mr. Reed. But if they can get that far at least it'll show we are in progress. And hope it will not trigger further assassinations.

"As I see it, I do believe we will get another messages putting a time limit on the passing of the demands. My reasoning comes from the fact that they extended a five year period for the currency exchange to gold and silver.

"Those who are heading-up this assault on our current election laws, I'm sure, are totally versed on what it takes to amend the Constitution, prepare a joint resolution and pass a bill into a law. But what we must do is to inform the American people about the processes and the time it takes.

"Schedule another press conference for Saturday May 17, at ten o'clock, after we have gone over the proposed demands, so I can advise the public to their step by step processes. I want to be seen all over the world, so be sure that all the visual media's cover the event. I'll need thirty minutes. I hope both Houses can agree on whatever demands brought before them so that I can relate that they are in the process of being considered. That also may buy us some more time.

"Reed, I'm sure that you realize, I not only want the American people to understand the tremendous strain these demands are upon this government, but I also want these so-called righteous assassins to realize what it is going to take to fulfill their demands. That's if both houses don't reject the demands and we get another massacre on their hands."

"Mr. President, I'll have my staff set it up as soon as I leave your office."

"Reed, why are you still here."

He smiled and I left.

CONGRESS PREPARES TO CONVENE:

I stayed abreast of the Senate's actions. Seven a.m. the following day, (May 16) the Majority Democratic Senate Leader Perry Weed took the lead seconds after the sound of the gavel and introduced the Bills and Joint Resolutions.

Explanation: (**The letters S. stands for Senate and the J. RES. Stands for Joint Resolution. Bills that begin with H.R. indicates a House Bill).**

The first step was taken. But, will it be enough to block out that dark shadow of death that's lurking over Washington? I'm sure the same thoughts crossed Stone's mind.

Washington was bussing like a disturbed bee hive. Every news broadcaster had a different slant on the events to come. The senators remain behind closed doors discussing their pros and cons on what they were to agree upon till almost one o'clock that afternoon.

When they finally began to enter the main chambers no one was talking. Grim faces casted their opinions as they paraded silently into the chamber.

One by one they settled in their seats. It was eerie. The usual picture is one of small groups huddling together planning their---whatever. Finally, the sound of the gavel and the meeting came to order. Senator Weed stepped up to the podium and related that there wasn't any time to have a committee or sub-committee hearings for any discussions or mark-ups. The bills, joint resolutions and Amendment changes were printed in a report. Both Houses have been separately assembled to eliminate time. He further announced that there wasn't time for a *conference* committee recommendations. These bills and Amendment changes must be passed or rejected today. He again reminded them that they weren't present for a debate. He then further explained that regardless of what is introduced and passed, in order for a proposed Constitutional Amendment change to become part of the Constitution it must be ratified by three-fourths of the States (38-50).

When it comes to passing a proposed bill into a law that takes only the signature of the President. Each bill and Amendment changes were described in detail and all that was heard were moans and groans. A roll call was taken after each reading. Ninety Senators were present the other ten were assassinated. The ten empty seats were a morbid reminder of why they were there!

Senator Weed began to read each document one by one.

Hours passed and the discussions with disagreements were lengthy. At five o'clock they took a dinner break and returned near seven o'clock. By eleven o'clock the Senators were ready to refer the proposed bills and Amendment changes to the House where it will follow the same routine of discussions and dissent. Some of them were amended. The changes were minor so they didn't need to be sent back to the Senate.

With the two-thirds approval of both Houses (this is accordance with Article V of the Constitution) the bills, joint resolutions and Amendment changes were ready to be sent to the President for his agreement. Now, according to the Constitution, the President actually does not play a role in the amendment process, except for his signature which is required so a bill can become a law, but he can't sign a joint resolution into a law. The forwarding of the proposed bills, joint resolutions and Amendment changes to the awaiting President was carried out immediately.

But, what still remains is the fact that each of the fifty States must vote to ratify the Joint Resolutions and amendments changes. This means that each State's Governor must receive the proposed amendment from the National Archives and Records Administration (NARA) connected to the Office of the Federal Register (OFR) and submit it to their State's Legislature for ratification. The OFR examines the ratification documents for their legal and authenticating signatures. The only way around this procedure is a **Constitutional Convention** which can be called by two-thirds of the State's Legislatures to convene. This has never been done before.

THE OVAL OFFICE RECEIVES THE PROPOSED AMENDMENTS

It was a few minutes passed three a.m. when the House forwarded the joint resolutions and bills with amendment changes to the Oval Office where the President was waiting with his staff and those he choose to have with him. By now the media was calling them the **Stone-6 Group.** It took twenty hours for the five bills and joint resolution Amendment changes to pass through both Houses.

During the long wait, the trouble between Israel and Palestine on the Gaza Strip began to escalate. The seven year blockade of the border was strangling the Palestinian population. No food causing starvation and no jobs to earn money if they had food.

Sometimes, I wonder if it was a wise movement in 1947, giving land near Jerusalem to the Israelites. It always seems, if you give certain people an inch, they want the whole twelve inches after a while. President Stone is smack dab in the middle over this issue.

The U. S. must avoid using military help to aid Israel, but still attempt to keep both sides from bringing total war to the Middle East. Of course, Iran is furnishing rockets to the Palestine and this countries' war mongers are selling weapons to Israel.

Israel controls three borders and their friendly allies, the Egyptians controls the other one. Thusly, locking-in the Palestinians. Oh, well its best that I get my mind back on this country's problem.

Now, it was the Presidents turn to go over the individual bills and joint resolutions and get them ratified as soon as possible. He better have a top hat full of Governor IOU rabbits. Reed was to read each joint resolution and bill in its entirety and the chosen guest were to agree or present their objections to certain issues, if any.

"Gentlemen, I'm not sure if each or any of you know the structure of a joint resolution. Each one will have its Proposal and Articles that are explained in Sections. They will be valid after they are ratified by the legislatures of three-fourths of the States of America (38 of 50) unless otherwise specified.

"Every bill has at least three parts: A **Preamble** which covers the reason for the bill. The **Body** should be separated into sections and subsections. Each proposed idea for the implementation of the bill should be a section. Subsections are used to provide further details and clarification or definitions for their appropriate bill section. And the third section should be the **Enactment Clause** which relates when the bill will take effect if passed. Any bills that deals with an Enactment date within 30 days of passage are considered for *Emergency Legislation* only.

"Now, the process to change an Amendment is quite different. It can be presented in the form of a joint resolution or a bill. The authority to amend the Constitution of the United States is derived from Article V of the Constitution. After Congress proposes an Amendment change, the Archivist of the United States, who heads the National Archives and Records Administration (NARA), is charged with the responsibility for administrating the ratification process under the provisions of 1U.S.C. 106b. The Archivist also collaborates with the Director of the Federal Register and they follow procedures and customs established by the previous Secretary of State and Administrator of General Services. If there are no questions, I'll begin? Silence was his answer.

It was a tad passed four a.m. when Reed began reading what both Houses forwarded to the Oval Office:

S.J.RES. 1 -- Proposing an amendment to the Constitution of the United States relative to limiting the number of years that a Member of Congress, a Member of the House of Representatives, all other elected officials to any office of the United States Government and the Upper and Lower courts, which includes the Supreme Court may serve to six years.

113th Congress -- 1st Session
In the Senate of the United States
May 16 (legislative day, May 16), 2014

The Senate and House of Representatives collectively introduced the following joint resolution; which was read and not referred to any committee.

JOINT RESOLUTION

Proposing an amendment to the Constitution of the United States relative to limiting the number of years that a Member of Congress, House of Representatives and all other elected to any office of the United States Government of Upper and Lower Courts, which includes the Supreme Court may serve.

Resolved by the Senate and House of Representatives of the United States of America in Congress assembled (two-thirds of each House concurring therein), that the following article is proposed as an amendment to the Constitution of the United States, which shall be valid to all intents and purposes as part of the Constitution when ratified by the legislatures of three-fourths of the States within 60 days after the date of its submission by Congress:

ARTICLE—

Section 1. No person can serve more than six years in a government office. If a vacancy occur, for any reason, after a person is elected, the position shall remain vacant until the term's end.

Section 2. No person shall have the right to be re-elected to any other office of the United States Government. Each elected person shall only serve one six year term.

Section 3. There shall be no Life-time terms to any office within the United States Government.

Section 4. There shall be no pensions or any other type of perks after leaving office.

Section 5. All present elected officials will finish out their present term and not seek re-election. They also shall not receive any pension or perks after leaving office under this article.

Section 6. The sole purposes of both Houses will be to use the power to benefit the American people through their passing of laws. This pertains especially to any treaties involving foreign trade.

Section 7. Filibustering is a "no-no". Majority rules. The benefits and the protections of the American people's health and welfare must prevail.

Section 8. Congress has have the power to implement and enforce this article by appropriate legislature.

"Gentlemen with all due respects to the above joint resolution, over the past two decades term limits has been one of the hottest debated topics across the nation. Americans are sick and tired of local politicians embedding themselves in an office waiting for a shot to run for Congress. Fifteen States have already voted overwhelmingly to place term limits on their state legislatures.

"Thirty-seven states presently place some form of term limits on their governors and other constitutional officers. And, popularity of the term limit laws has remained in each state that has passed such laws. The future generations of young politicians are very worried about more states passing term limit laws.

"Furthermore, presently nine of the ten largest cities in America have term limits for their city council and for mayors. So, this joint resolution will be a most popular one.

"The next bill is in conjunction to the term limits joint resolution.

Committee: Senate   Principal Author: Perry Weed
Bill # S.2650   Delegation: Senate & House of Representatives
Title of Bill Benefits and Compensation.
An Act to Reduce Favoritism, Entrenchment, Patronage and Government's Budget.

1. **Preamble:** Whereas a base salary with no increases during the term and no
2. pension or perks after leaving office. Government provided health insurance and
3. mandatory retirement at age 70 years. Let it be pure and clear there shall be no
4. life-time tenures in any office.
5. Section 1: This Act to be cited as, "Term Limits and Benefits Bill".
6.   Sub-Section B: Salary $100,000.00 with no increases.
7.   Sub-Section C: No re-election or Life-time tenure.
8.   Sub-Section D: No pension or perks after leaving office.
9.   Sub-Section E: Be present in the Senate Chambers 180 days a year.
10.   Sub-Section F: No salaries or bonuses for committee work.
11. Section 2: Office and Expenses when needed and approved by Budget Committee.
12.   Sub-Section A: Expense proposals submitted monthly.
13. Section 3: Legislative Aides.
14.   Sub-Section A: Appointed by the White House Employment Office.
15.   Sub-Section B: No Aide to be furnished by an outside organization.
16. Section 4: This bill shall go into effect immediately.
     Reed finished with, "Any comments gentlemen?"

The President commented with, "I'm sure that some refinements with be forthwith.

Continue Mr. Reed."
 Reed picked-up the second joint resolution and began:

S.J.RES. 2 – Proposing an amendment to the Constitution of the United States relating to donations, contributions, expenditures and campaigning time periods for any elected government office intended to affect elections.
113th Congress – 1st Session
In the Senate of the United States
May 16 (legislative day, May 16), 2014
The Senate and the House of Representatives collectively introduce the following joint resolution; which was read and not referred to any committee.
JOINT RESOLUTION
Proposing an amendment to the Constitution of the United States relating to donations, contributions, expenditures and campaigning time periods for any elected government office intended to affect elections.

Resolved by the Senate and the House of Representatives of the United States of America in Congress assembled (two-thirds of each house concurring therein), that the following article is proposed as an amendment to the Constitution of the United States, which shall be valid to all intents and purposes as part of the Constitution when ratified by the legislatures of three-fourths of the States within 60 days after the date of its submission by Congress:
ARTICLE –
    Section 1. To concur with the fundamental principal of political equality for all elected officials, no Congress, House of Representatives or any other government office shall have the right to except cash or any other form of donations, contributions, expenditures for campaigning or so-called "running for office."
    Section 2. Each Candidate competing between two opposite political parties will receive from the United States Government (paid through donations from the countries tax payers via their income tax statement) the sum of $100,000.00.
    Section 3. Each candidate can use an additional $25,000.00 from their own funds.
    Section 4. Each candidate will receive an equal allotted time television time within their own State, which will also be paid for by the United States Government. Said time to be ten hours no matter how many commercials that can be allotted in that time frame.
    Section 5. Campaigning time period will begin no sooner than six months prior to the day of the casting of votes/ballots and cease that day thereof.
    Section 6. It shall also be construed that any other media, newspaper, television station shall not donate, give free air or print time to any candidate.
    Section 7. Any candidate found in violation of this law will be automatically be removed from the election ballot and forfeit any opportunity to be elected.
    Section 8. Congress shall have the power to implement and enforce this article by appropriate legislation.
    Reed waited for a few seconds before beginning reading the next joint resolution. As he finished reading the resolution number he stopped and said, "I'm not quite sure if everyone in the room is familiar with the group called Citizens United and what the Supreme Court's ruling **Citizens United v. Federal Election Commission** did to help destroy the voting process of this country.
    "Citizens United is a Political Action Committee (PAC) founded in 1988, and was funded by the Cove Brothers. It has become a very sad reality of our society. It represents the ambitions of the rich elite, corporate America and unions and is hell bend on destroying this country's form of being a Republic or a Democracy. Now, it's quite easy to forget how

to distinguish the differences between the two. And, truthfully, most citizens of this country don't realize that there is a difference. So, please allow me the time to explain the differences.

"The chief or key, if you will, difference between a **democracy** and a **republic** lies in the limits placed on government by law, which has implications on minority rights. Both forms of government use a **representational system** where citizens vote to elect politicians to represent their interests and form the government.

"However, in a **republic**, a constitution or charter of rights protects certain inalienable rights that cannot be taken away by government, even if it has been elected by a majority of voters. In a pure **democracy**, the majority is not restrained and can impose its will on the minority. This America is supposed to be a **Republic.**

"Ok, back to the Supreme Court's decision and the harm it has done. Let me take it back to the year 1907. That year Congress passed the Titman Act, which banned corporations from funding federal election campaigns. The Tart-Harley Act, in 1947, extended the ban to labor unions. But, unfortunately the laws were weak and tough to enforce. More help came in 1971, when Congress passed the Federal Election Campaign Act, which required full reporting of campaign contributions and expenditures. It also limited spending on media advertisements. But it was eventually ruled unconstitutional.

"The January 21st 2010, Supreme Court's ruling overturned the campaign finance laws. The court overturned two existing Supreme Court decisions of "**electioneering communications"** (Austin V. Michigan Chamber of Commerce and McConnell V. FEC). By striking down these decisions they unleased unlimited corporate and union spending in not just federal candidate campaigns, but allows for millions to be spent to influence state and local elections where money is very effective.

"Reversing the laws is a radical attack on the American political system and poses grave dangers to the integrity of this country. So, that brings me to the next joint resolution.

S.J.RES. 3 – Proposing an amendment to the Constitution of the United States to restore the rights of the American people that were taken away by the Supreme Court's decision in the Citizens United V. Federal Election Commission and related decisions, to protect the integrity of our elections, and to limit the corrosive influence of money in our voting process.

113th Congress – 1st Session
In the Senate of the United States
May 16 (legislative day, May 16), 2014

The Senate and the House of Representatives collectively introduce the following joint resolution; which was read and nor referred to any committee.

JOINT RESOLUTION

Proposing an amendment to the Constitution of the United States to restore the rights of the American people that were taken away by the Supreme Court's decision in the Citizens United V. Federal Election Commission and related decisions, to protect the integrity of our elections, and to limit the corrosive influence of money in our voting process.

Resolved by the Senate and House of Representatives of the United States of America in Congress assembled (two-thirds of each House concurring therein), that the following article is proposed as an amendment to the Constitution of the United States, which shall be valid to all intents and purposes as part of the Constitution when ratified by legislatures of three-fourths of the States within 60 days after the date of its submission by Congress:

ARTICLE –

Section 1. Whereas this amendment shall overturn the Supreme Court's decisions and restore the right to vote in public elections belongs <u>only</u> to natural persons as citizens of the United States, so shall the ability to make contributions through their income tax forms, which the amount will be set by Congress during this session.

Section 2. Nothing in this amendment shall be construed to restrict the power of Congress to protect the integrity and fairness of the voting process, limit the corrupting influence of private wealth in public elections.

Section 3. Be it clear that the freedom of the press, media's or any other advertising companies, corporations, institutions and any sources of advertisement is limited to written opinions equal to all political parties. Equality in expression by all advertising media's is at point.

Section 4. Any violation of this law is subject to sanctions, fines and imprisonment by Congress.

Section 5. Congress shall have the power to implement and enforce this article by appropriate legislature.

"Well, gentlemen, I think that joint resolution is as plain as the nose on one's face."

Reed paused and sipped from a bottle of water before reading the next joint resolution.

"This next joint resolution deals with the process of selecting the electors in each state and their responsibilities. Please bear with me while I go over the procedures.

"The citizens of the United States <u>do not</u> elect their president directly. When an eligible voter cast his or her ballot they are really voting for an elector. This elector is pledged to vote for that same candidate. Of course, this leave the door open to many types of manipulations of which a few have been used in the past.

"There are 538 such electors, as a group they are called the Electoral College. It takes One-half of the total number of votes plus one, or 270. I'm sure a few in this room are in favor of abolishing this system. Now, having explained the process, I'll continue.

S.J.RES. 4 – Proposing an amendment to the Constitution of the United States to abolish the Electoral College and to provide for the direct popular election of the President and Vice-President of the United States.

113th Congress – 1st Session
In the Senate of the United States
May 16 (legislative day, May 16), 2014
The Senate and the House of Representatives collectively introduce the following Joint resolution; which was read and not referred to any committee.
JOINT RESOLUTION

Proposing an amendment to the Constitution of the United States to abolish the Electoral College and to provide for the direct popular election of the President and Vice-President of the United States.

Resolved by the Senate and the House of Representatives of the United States of America in Congress assembled (two-thirds of each House concurring therein), that the following article is proposed as an amendment to the Constitution of the United States, which shall be valid to all intents and purposes as part of the Constitution when ratified by the legislatures of three-fourths of the States within 60 days after the date of its submission by Congress:

ARTICLE –

Section 1. The President and the Vice-President shall be elected by the majority vote of the people.

Section 2. The persons having the greatest number of votes for President and Vice-President shall be elected, if such number is at least 1 % greater than any opposing candidate. (Example: 100 million votes cast—1% =10,000 votes). If no person shall have such a number, a runoff election shall be held 30 days after the general election. In a runoff election, the choice of President and Vice-President shall be made from the persons who received the two highest numbers of votes for each office in the general election?

Section 3. The times, places, and manner of holding such elections, and entitlement to inclusion on the ballot for the general election, shall be prescribed by Congress and not each State. Congress shall also have the power to ascertain and declare the results of such elections.

Section 4. Names of candidates shall not be joined unless they shall have consented thereto and no candidate shall consent to his or her name being joined with that of more than one other person.

Section 5. Congress shall have the power to implement and enforce this article by appropriate legislation.

As Reed was about to continue, the President interrupted with, "Gentlemen, Mr. Reed is an authority on the history of our government and it was at my suggestion that he refreshed us all in these matters. I sorry for the interruption Mr. Reed, please continue".

"In May of 1787, in the town of Philadelphia, PA., delegates of twelve of the original thirteen colonies convened to prepare a Constitution which would consist of two chambers, a Senate and a House of Representatives. It was called the Constitutional Convention. I won't go into the lengthy months of debates only what was finally decided after almost four months of argumentative remedies.

"The original idea was to have a single national legislating government structured with each state having a Senate and a House of Representatives. No matter how large or small in population, each would have only two seats. This caused quite a bit of chaos because the larger populated states figured they were bigger and should have more people to represent them than the smaller populated states. So eventually, they came up with what became known as the "*Great Compromise"* because the debates were threatening to derail the entire convention.

"This compromise became a solution to their problem my structuring a Bicameral structure with an **Upper House** with two seat per state and the **Lower House** with its seat in proportion to its population. It was called ***Proportional Representation.*** This is when the ten year census was created.

"The two chambers were meant to emphasis the benefits of *checks and balances.* By dividing the power this was supposed to prevent either from having tyrannical power. Of course, it didn't work. The current system, which is realized by many, is inadequate. Article V of the Constitution stops or gives the right to amend the Constitution.

"In 1789, the House had 65 members, and in 1913, it had 435 and remained at that number until Hawaii and Alaska became states (437). It was eventually capped by the ***Public law #62-5 aka The Apportionment Act of 1911*** at 435.

"And today each state uses what is called **Gerrymandering** which has goals of **Packing and Cracking** to maximize the effect of supporter's votes and to minimize the effect of opponents' votes. Its common name is "redistricting".

"In my belief, all this country needs is one house to suggest, create, review and pass laws pertaining to the benefit of the people and the country and not to anyone's or any business organization's monetary benefits. Both Houses are redundant institutions which quagmire this country's forward movements.

"I suppose my words might make some of think that I sympathetic toward the demands of this assassins group. I just know our great country is going in the wrong direction and somehow or way it must be stopped. Well, enough said. I'll read the next bill, which goes hand in hand with the **S.J.RES. 4 joint resolution.**

Committee: Senate   Principal Author: Perry Weed

Bill # S.2651   Delegation: Senate & House of Representatives
Title of Bill or Joint Resolution: Gerrymandering or the Re-districting of States and
Changes to the Bicameral Structure of Congress.

1. **Preamble:** Whereas the number of Representative in the House must be reduced
2. to two members per State. Thusly, giving each State no matter the number of its
3. population equal representation. Furthermore, halt any State in changing or altering
4. their voting districts to benefit a candidate of any party. This will change the Bicameral
5. Structure of Congress and be in accordance with the new elected official's terms in
6. office. Article V provides for making amendments to the Constitution
7. This is meant to be in accordance with the 15 th and 19 th Amendments. The 15
8. gave the right to ever person no matter of skin color to vote and the 19 enfranchised women with the right to vote.
9. This ruling will also end the practices of ***Packing & Cracking*** which are the goals of
10. ***Gerrymandering.***
11. Section 1: Reduce the number of each State's Representatives to two per state no
12.   matter of the size of its population. Proportional Representation.
13.   Sub-Section A: Two per State equally a total of 100.
14. Section 2: Eliminate Re-Districting, aka; Packing and Cracking.
15.   Sub-Section A: Each State will their current school Districts for voting
16.   Districts.
17.   Sub-Section B: Thusly, eliminating the Gerrymandering goals of
18.   maximizing the efforts of any one party's effect of support
19.   voters, and minimizing the effect of opponent's votes.
20. Section 3: This bill shall go into effect immediately.

    Reed waited again for someone to speak. He looked around in amazement and said, "I don't understand your silence, gentlemen. Three Joint resolutions and two bill read and nothing from the Peanut gallery?"

     Reed was about to continue when the President said, "Mr. Reed, I believe we're all waiting till the end of the last joint resolution and bill to voice an opinion. Please continue."

     "Mr. President, I think it's time for a refreshment break. Please let's open the bar for a brief breather."

     "As you wish Mr. Reed." Was the President's answer.

     I know damn sure that I needed some white lighting. You could a couple of sighs of relief. It took more than one belt to settle the anxiety

    It was about fifteen minutes after four a.m. before I started too resumed. I didn't get a chance to utter a word when General Josh White butted in and said, "I can realize why this terrorist group wants to change Congress. The U.S. Congress is a national disgrace and are being ruled and led by big oil and gas corporations, the insurance industry, the pharmaceutical and medical profession. If history will have its way, they will eventually fail, but by then, so too will the nation. This country is nothing but a large herd of sheep and those companies are the black sheep with the bell leading us into a slaughter by the Middle East terrorist groups. One by one they are created by the wealthy elite using our very own CIA and other covert organizations. Up until a year ago nobody ever heard of ISIS. They invent the terrorist names and groups at will to confuse the American citizen. Damn it, why don't this country wake up to that fact that the very core of this government is corrupt! And it needs to live with it or bite the bullet and make the proper changes.

     "It began in 1997, with Abu-Nidal Organization, Hamas, Jihad, Boko Haram, Al-Queda, Hezbollah, Army of Islam, Sunnis, Shiite and now Isis to name a few. What we should be doing is spending more money in building-up our armed forces and weaponry. Each male and female should serve at least one year in the Army, Navy, Marine or any other branch of the military. This will really give us the mightiest military forces in the world.

"These young people need the proper training and respect for their country and there is no better way than in any branch of the military to learn disciplined and weaponry training at an early age. Well, I said my piece. Thank you Mr. Reed for allowing me to express my opinion. It want it very clear, on this issue, that a strong military would solve this problem."

"Does anyone else want to have their say at this time? No. Then I'll continue. The next Joint resolution pertains to a national voter's card.

"But first let me bring in the history of this very important item. It may be a little boring, but I believe it and the other histories of these bills and joint resolutions are necessary. It simply is to get everyone, in this room, off the political hanging hook. Whatever decisions made in this room are going to become a matter of record because everything said here today is being recorded. Ok, with that said, I'll begin. Reed pick-up his notes.

"In 1787, the passage of the Constitution gave white male property owners age 21 and older the right to vote. Then between 1807 and 1843, a series of changes took place with the main one being that all white men 21 and older could vote.

"Then in February of 1870, the 40th Congress created the 15th Amendment which guaranteed that all men that were 21 or older regardless of race or ethnic background had the right to vote. Following that in 1920, the 19th Amendment gave women age 21 and older the right to vote.

"Greed reared its head and some States were charging a pole tax, which was mainly directed at the very poor and the colored race. So in 1964, the 24th Amendment made it illegal to charge a poll tax to voters.

"In 1965, the Voting Rights Act authorized the federal government to take over the registration of voters because there were states preventing people of color and other minorities from registering to vote or cast their ballots through the usage of literacy tests, grandfather clauses, and intimidation tactics. This Act enforced provisions previously guaranteed in the 13th, 14th, and 15th Amendments.

"In 1971, the 26th Amendment lowered the voting age across the nation to 18 years of age. In 1982, the Voting Rights Act was further amended to include Americans with disabilities, voters not able to read or write and those who were not fluent in the English language to vote.

"And, finally, in 1993, The National Registration Act expanded the polling places to be convenient for all registered voters. The departments of Safety, Health, Human Services, Mental Health and Retardation, Veteran's Affairs, Libraries, Post Offices, County Clerks Offices, and the Registrar of Deeds were all to make voter forms available to the public.

"That being said, I'll begin the next joint resolution.

S.J. RES. -- 5 Proposing an amendment to the Constitution of the United States relating to a National and Federal voting card, voter age, registration places and how it will be initiated.

113th Congress – 1st Session
In the Senate of the United States
May 16 (legislative day May 16), 2014

The Senate and the House of Representatives collectively introduce the following joint resolution; which was read and not referred to any committee.

JOINT RESOLUTION

Proposing an amendment to the Constitution of the United States relating to a National and Federal voting card, voter age, registration places, and how it will be initiated.

Resolved by the Senate and House of Representatives of the United States of America in Congress assembled (two-thirds of each House concurring therein), that the following article is proposed as an amendment to the Constitution of the United States, which shall be valid to all intents and purposes as part of the Constitution when ratified by the legislatures of three-fourths of the States within 60 days after the date of its submission
By Congress:
ARTICLE –

Section 1. Pursuant to and from the passage of the Constitution in 1787, the changes between 1807 through 1843, the 15th, 19th, 24th, the Voting Rights Act of 1965, the 26th Amendment , its extensions in 1982, and the 1993, National Voter Registration Act additions of voters registration places will remain as they were intended with the except of the following Sections.

Section 2. The new language that is be written into this new amendment will not include any and all power each state had pertaining to voters rights and places.

Section 3. This amendment only allows the federal government through Congress to amend or change any part of this amendment.

Section 4. All legal American citizens age 18 and older, no matter of race, creed color, disabilities, either physical or mental shall be eligible to vote in federal, state and local elections, providing they have registered to vote and produce a valid Voters Registration Card according to the articles of this amendment.

Section 5. All States of America will ratify this amendment or be monetarily sanctioned by the removal of any and all aide from the federal government until ratified.

Section 6. A new picture voter identification card will be issued to all eligible American citizen providing they have citizenship proof in the form of a birth certificate, current passport, citizenship papers, and their current local voter's card. No immigration papers, green card, letter of entry will be accepted.

Section 7. A felony convicted criminal must reapply for his or her right to obtain a voter's card. No exceptions. Re-submission forms will be obtained from parole officers.

Section 8. There will be a fifteen day early voting time in all federal state and local elections.

Section 9. Each state and the District of Columbia, Washington D.C. will provide locations for the procurement of Federal Voters Cards, voter's registration, ballot casting places. Said places shall be, but not limited to, Driver License offices, Libraries, Post Offices and Court Houses.

Section 10. This article shall take effect following ratification, but allow one year for all States and the District of Columbia, Washington D.C. implement these facilities.

"The next answer to the demand to return to the gold and silver standard is not in a form of a joint resolution or a bill, but an ***open letter to the demanders.*** It reads:

'We, the undersigned need time to debate and confer with many other nations before a drastic change is made to the United States currency system. We, agree that the dollar has been under close scrutiny from many countries. The global currencies are vastly disconnected and poorly rated. World trade hinging on the dollar is slowly losing its popularity for payment. But, is a gold and silver standard the right one?

'There are those who hold that the Constitution should be interpreted very strictly and believe the Federal Reserve System and paper money are unconstitutional. The Congress wasn't granted the specific power to create a central bank. Therefore, the Federal Reserve is unconstitutional. The federal government has only the power to mint gold and silver coins and not paper money.

'Also, no Nation, as of 2013, uses a gold and silver standard as a basis of its monetary system even though they may hold substantial gold and silver reserves. The Federal

Reserve System of 1913, President Roosevelt's Banking Act of 1935, the Federal Open Market Committee and the Monetary Control Act of 1980, have made many changes to our monetary system. Some good and some bad.

'As of March 2014, the International Monetary Fund (IMF) is proposing to use a system it created in 1969 called the **SPECIAL DRAWING RIGHTS (SDR's)** as an international reserve asset monetary system to support the expansion of the growing world trade.

'The SDR is neither a currency, nor a claim on the IMF. Rather, it is a potential claim on the freely usable currencies of IMF members.

'The IMF believes the SDR's can supplement its member countries' official reserves. Its value is based on a basket of four key international currencies: the Euro, Japanese Yen, Pound Sterling and the U.S. dollar. Enough on that subject. We can let both Houses debate the changing of this country's monetary system.

'In conclusion, we, ask for the five year time period to attempt to eliminate, merge, undo, alter or create a new monetary system for America and possibly the world.'

At that, Mr. Reed said, "The **open letter** is signed by all ninety Senators and it brings us to the closed of five Joint Resolutions and two Bills. Its fifteen minutes passed five and we have one hour for any comments, good or bad. So, who'll take the floor?"

The President opened with, I would like to hear from my added guests first, if no one minds? Mr. Holden, please your comments."

Holden stirred in his chair before saying, "Gentlemen, I believe most government employees really don't know what it actually takes to pass a bill. But, of course that's not the case at point. When a bill or joint resolution is to be passed it must first be referred to the appropriate committee, of which there are presently,17 Senate committees, with 70 subcommittees, and 23 House committees, with 104 subcommittees for review. What has to be done here and now is to satisfy the demands is to step over the long process and place the responsibility for this crisis in the President's lap. Because, no matter what Congress does, the disgrace to this nation of the last 12 days was on his watch. The history books may not be kind to his name, then again, they may reflect the views of the people that elected him to lead this great country.

"In the 2000 election, this country's government was taken over by a group of politicians with only one goal in mind, to control the world by means of whatever it took. Since that time, in the estimation of the people whom elected our President, he has done almost everything he had promised for **'change'** and, I might add, against insurmountable odds.

"I personally agree with the demands because it's a tragic shame that the most blessed nation, the United States, is completely subjugated by so few. Why? Because our government as it stands today is in grave trouble of going the way of other ancient societies of the past. There are two major problems deeply entrenched in our Congress: The root of them is the greed of the very few elite and our monetary system.

"We, the voters and non-voters allowed money to buy, obtain, and swindle us to sticking our heads in the sand when it came to political campaign promises. But, salvation is ahead in elections being held in 2015. The Congress of this Nation is about to change with term limits. It will give us, the voters, the ability to clean **house** in both chambers, and as an added boon cut the federal budget from the bloat they have created for themselves.

"Term limits of elected officials dates back to the American Revolution which was also referred to as **rotation in office.** Term limits were incorporated into the Articles of Confederation (1781-1789). George Mason, an American Statesman and Patriot said in 1788: 'Nothing is as essential to the preservation of a Republic government as a periodic rotation.' (We have sure screwed that up).

"Secondly, reign in the banking industry and shut down the thievery of Wall Street by abolishing the Federal Reserve System. The Fed's operate on three false premises. The sole purpose of creating the Fed System was to prevent depressions, stabilize currency, and protect the people's bank accounts (deposits and checking) in the nation's banks. The Founding Fathers originally recognized the enemies of a sound money system and the Fed's contain all three of them:

"First was to avoid turning over to any group of private bankers the right to print the official currency of the nation. To quote Thomas Jefferson, he wrote: **'If the American people ever allow private banks to control the issue of currency, first by inflation, then by deflation, the banks and corporations that will grow around them will deprive the people of all property until their children will wake up homeless on the continent their fathers conquered.' (Quoted in ibid, p. 247.)**

"And another great man, Abraham Lincoln also warned the nation about private bankers after the National Bank Act was passed in 1863, he wrote: **'I see in the near future a crisis approaching that unnerves me and cause me to tremble for the safety of my country. Corporations (of banking) have been enthroned, an era of corruption in high places will follow, and the money power of the country will endeavor to prolong its reign by working upon the prejudices of the people, until the wealth is aggregated in a few hands and the Republic destroyed.' (Quoted in ibid, p. 9.)**

"The second deception is charging for printing and borrowing the country's own currency. The fed's demand that all U.S. currency be printed as Federal Reserve notes. But, if the government wants to use these notes it must give the Fed's interest bearing IOU's in form of government bonds and pay said interest until the bonds are redeemed.

'So, the government pays the Fed's to print their own money or Federal Reserve notes, but don't forget the notes are not backed by gold, silver or anything of value. They're just paper notes, backed by virtually nothing.

"Now, you think why are they able to charge the government interest when all they are doing is just printing the government's own money. To explain that we'll have to take a trip back in time to 1913, when the Federal Reserve Act was forced through Congress during Woodrow Wilson's Presidency.

"Congress during Christmas time (almost every Senator was gone) passed the Act giving the newly created Federal Reserve the *right* to print the government's money. Therefore, if the government wants the Fed's to print money it has to borrow it and give the Fed's IOUs in the form of interest bearing bonds for the amount obtained. And, that bill was tagged with a tax in the form of the people's income tax to pay interest on the bonds.

"Even Wilson had regrets with the passing of the Act. He later said, 'I am a most unhappy man. *I have unwittingly ruined my country.* A great industrial nation is controlled by its system of credit. Our system of credit is concentrated. The growth of the nation, therefore, and all our activities are in the hands of a few men. We have come to be one of the worst ruled, one of the most completely controlled and dominated governments in the civilized world. No longer a government by free opinion, no longer a government by conviction and the vote of the majority, but a government by the opinion and duress of a small group of dominant men.'

"Well, hells bells. The U.S. government, by the right of the Constitution, has the right to create money, why should it borrow its own money from the Fed's and give them interest bearing bonds or IOU's in exchange for their own money, which becomes a debt upon the country's citizens.

"The third con is a real law breaker. It is a fraud to loan, rent, or sell something which doesn't exist. In banking terms it's called *fractional banking.* How that works is it allows a bank to set up a **reserve** to cover any claims (demand for deposit withdrawal) which happens to come in, and then go ahead and loan many times more money on credit than the **reserve** in the bank. Actually, what this means is that the bank loans out and charges interest on considerable **money it doesn't even have**.

"Example: A bank receives a $100 dollar deposit and immediately creates a $100 dollar IOU. It keeps 20 % ($20 dollars) in reserve and loans out $80 dollar to a customer. Its money supply immediately becomes $180 dollars to loan out.

"The word for fractional banking is **E*ndogeny*** which means ***growth from within.*** Oh, and one more important banking term: ***Bailment*** which is what banks call a customer's cash or check deposit. Why? Because these funds become the bank's property and it's no longer the depositor's. All you get is a fractional IOU.

"Thank you Mr. President for allowing me to give forth my opinion and beliefs."

"You're quite welcome. Does either of my senior advisors wish to give forth their thoughts on the matter?"

Jane Moore looked at her partner Dan Griff. Griff nodded to give Ms. Moore the ok to speak. She began with, "Thank you Mr.; President and gentlemen for allowing Dan and myself be part of this most crucial moment in our country's history. There are so many flaws in our way of legislation it just might take a person's life time to correct the damage the lust for greed and power that's embedded in almost every department of our government. Yet, an opportunity has presented itself via murder and mayhem.

"I realize that may sound a bit gross, but it is true. We as humans have only one fear and that is fear itself. There is no immortality, we do not return after death in another form. Oh, I don't mean to imply that there isn't a God or a creator of the universe. Each person of this planet or in the vast universe has a right to honor or pray and believe in someone or thing. It's what one can do to benefit our fellow citizens in this country and every other country or nation of this world that really counts.

"Our founding Fathers came to this country to get away from oppression and a one-sided society. They wanted freedom and equality for all. We have a second chance to correct the wrongs of a corrupt government. If we don't change, now that we are given, no forced, to change what is going to happen to the un-born children of the future? Do we want history to record our failure to do what is right?

"President Stone you are also one of those that will leave an office in 2016. You have the time and the power of the people to make these demand changes. How about the un-mentioned changes to issues that are also absolutely necessary, such as, protecting this nation's clean water rights, immigration laws, stopping billions of dollar subsidies for the oil and drug companies to name a few. America badly needs a new tax code that will be equally fair for the people, companies and corporations.

"Well, thank you gentlemen for allowing Mr. Griff and myself to present our views."

She hadn't got the last word out when my cell phone started to vibrate. I looked at my wrist watch, it was ten minutes to six. I turned around and walked toward the far wall to take the call.

CHAPTER SIX
THE FIFTH MESSAGE

It was my Associated Press news source in the New York City office. They just received a new message. It came over the wire service from their APTN London office and addressed to the President of the United States. He read the message: ***One giant step for mankind. Be warned! Continue or more will fall!***

He related that it was hacked into their London's office news teletype machine. They are forwarded it to my office machine and are attempting to track where it originated and hung-up. I just stood there staring out across the room at the President. He sensed something was wrong and walk over to me and said, "Reed, what is it?"

"Mr. President, we have another message from our boogieman, Zapata. It's strange. I'll get the copy from my office and return directly."

It took about eight minutes. In the time that I was gone the President had told the group about the call. Handing the message to him, I stepped back and waited for him to speak.

"Ms. Moore and gentlemen, I'll read the twelve word message,"

After reading the last word, he set the message down. Silence and faces with question marks were the only answer.

My thoughts were how in the world could this be happening? Is this room bugged? No, of course not. It's swept every day and was just prior to this meeting. This is the second message sent via the AP. It's not going to be easy for AP to track the origin of the message because they have 243 news bureaus in 120 countries.

It was probably hacked into one of those bureaus and forwarded to their London Office. Hell, it could have been originated right here in D.C. It's unbelievable what a hacker can butt into and transmit. Well, I'll let Sunday and Domel worry about it.

The president only has four hours before his news conference. A couple hours of sleep, if he can, and then address the ragging bulls of the press. I wonder if he will tell them about this latest message. I know everyone in this building will know in a matter of ten minutes and that means it will leak out to the press.

Next, I said, "Mr. President, it's time to end our meeting, you need rest before your ten o'clock press conference."

Everyone exchanged their good-byes and I watched the President leave through the door leading to the family's private suite before I took my leave.

Before entering my office, I instructed my secretary to buss me in two hours. I also needed some shut-eye.

10:00 O'clock PRESS CONFERENCE

I arrived at the pressroom a bit beyond 9:30. Everything seemed ready for the President. Precisely at ten a.m., President Stone entered the room from the side door with his security guards. He was announced.

"The President of the United States."

Reaching the podium he looked out over the seated reporters and after a few moments he said, "Good morning, ladies and gentlemen. I will not be taking any questions after I have concluded. The White House press secretary, Mr. Brad James will allow a short question and answer session. I'll be brief in my assumption of Congress's laborious twenty hours putting together the joint resolutions and bills it will take to satisfy the demands of the assassins.

"I'm saddened by the events over the past twelve days. No other President in the history of this country has had to face this type of aggression. Our government is being held hostage, but not by terrorist. I believe they consider themselves patriots or if you will, champions of the people. The newspapers of this country will get the results of the action Congress has taken in this matter. Every demand has been met to make certain that no more deaths will occur.

"I have instructed that very State ratify these laws, not the customary three-fourths of the States (38 of 50). Since, I do not have the authority to sign these documents into law they must be forwarded to the National Archives and Records Administration (NARA), who is charged with the responsibility for administrating the ratification process after Congress proposes an amendment. Then, the original documents are forwarded directly to the Office of Federal Register (OFR) for publication and then sent to each State.

"Next, the Governor of each State convenes their State's Legislative bodies and they reject or ratify the amendment according to the will of the people of that State. This is precisely where our elected system has broken down. They no longer pass laws in favor of the people, but in favor of the rich elite, big businesses or wherever their campaign money comes from. That's why I going on record stating that I have admittedly insisted that every State ratify these joint resolutions and bills.

"I personally, look upon this opportunity as a second chance for the people of this country to regain their power of voting rights. It's the Constitutional right of every legal citizen over the age of eighteen to exercise their opinion at the ballot polls. And, no, I do not agree with the methods used to bring this crisis about.

"Every agency of this government is in process of trying to locate and capture these assassins. They hopefully will be routed out as soon as possible. Of course, I can't divulge any thing pertaining to their investigations at this time. But, I assure you they are using every method at their disposal in doing whatever it is going to take to apprehend these assassins.

"Each of you were given copies of the original demand note, the joint resolutions and bills prepared by both Houses and my today's statement. Now, for one final point on the importance of these demands being ratified. A fifth message was received in London's Associated Press office addressed to me early this morning. Please, realize the parties responsible for these assassinations are fully aware of what is taking place almost before they happen. I caution the Governors of each State to be prudent. This last message is another threat should Governors not do the bidding of the people of this country. On the monitor above my head you can see the message. It reads: *One giant step for mankind. Be warned! Continue or more will fall!*

"Thank you and God bless America."

The President exited accompanied by his bodyguards. Mr. James stepped up to the podium. And said, "Do not expect me to guess what the President is doing or going to do. I will allow six questions. I'll give you ten minutes to select the questions and the persons to ask them.

The task was done and only one person was selected to present the questions. It was Susan Buzton the AP's chief bureau Washington reporter. Her first question:

"Does the President believe there will be more demands?"

Answer. "If you read the next to the last paragraph in the original demand note it states, 'other changes will be recommended. Next question."

"Is there an internal White House investigation on going?"

Answer. "Yes. Next question."

"How many have been assassinated thus far?"

Answer. "Twenty-three. Next question."

"Does the President expect a problem with any of the Governors for the ratification process?"

Answer. "I can't answer that question. All of you know the temperaments and politics of the Governors. Next question."

"If the laws aren't ratified by all the Governors, what will President Stone do?"

Answer. "Only time will tell. Last question."

"Why does the President think the assassins are Champions of the people?"

Answer. "President Stone said, 'he thought that they perceived themselves in that manner. That concludes our question and answer session. Thank you all."

GOVERNOR'S REBILLION

Brad James stepped away from the podium and quickly exited. On his way back to the Oval Office he was stopped by Dan Steele, the chief of Staff. He was carrying the latest approval poll by Gallop. It gave President Stone an eighty-three percent approval relating on how he is handling this crisis. It was eleven fifteen a.m. when I arrived at the Situation Room. President Stone was seated listening to his watch teams bringing him up to speed on the reactions of this crisis around the world and other bad situations.

I hesitated and listened to the various team leaders relate the ISIS and ISIL situations. These two are separate in their controlled areas. ISIS (Islamic State in Iraq and Syria) and ISIL (Islamic State in Iraq and the Levant (Regions of Jordon, Israel, Lebanon, Cyrus, and Southern Turkey). The video of the beheading of an American newspaper correspondent was staring to stir-up some Senators requesting "boots on the ground" to combat these terrorist. They are trying to get the President to break his promise of "no war."

Russia seemed on the verge of invading the Ukraine, the unrest in the streets Ferguson, Mo., Syria becoming most violent with its Muslim terrorist organizations getting ready to use their chemical weapons stockpile, more Russian sanctions on the table, East Africa's Somalia's militant leader, Ahmed Abdi Godane is killed, Pakistan nuclear threat by the Provincially Administered Tribal Areas (PATA) remains volatile and the latest news from the Feds about the gap between the rich and poor in America is widening.

I couldn't help thinking, I'm glad it's him and not me in the Oval Office. On top of America's involvement around the globe, he still has the uncertainty of fifty Governors to contend with. It was well after four p.m. when the President took his leave and I slowly walked back to my office.

I no sooner sat down when my hot line rang. It was my contact in the Director of the National Governor's Association, Joyce Web. I was informed that Governor Cote Gaker had contacted several other State Governors to have their legislatures veto all the demands. He specifically talked to his four rat-pals, Governor, Rod Dingal, Governor, John Cork. Governor, Pete Gage, and Governor, Dell Thall.

Governor Gaker is a staunch bought and paid for Republican puppet. He's the type of low-life Governor that will bend down and kiss the *you know what* back-side of either one of the two Cove brothers. He and his other pals have caused problems in their States with voter's rights, Stonecare Health Program. Gaker was suspected of taking illegal campaign donations. He got lucky in a recall election and has generally been a big pain in the President's butt with his influence and fox News rhetoric at Governor's Forums.

I'll have to inform President Stone in the morning about his interference. He sure as hell didn't need any more problems on his plate of crisis situations. That night was a restless one for me and I can assume for the President also. I had just finished my second cup of coffee when my hall clock chimed, it was nine thirty. Rising, there was a knock at my residence's door. I wondered, who in the hell in DC has the audacity to come to my private home without an invitation?

I eyeballed the person through the door peephole. It was a uniformed AP messenger. Upon opening the door, he handed me a sealed envelope and immediately spun around and took his leave without saying a word. It seemed a bit strange.

Standing in the opened doorway, I slit the envelope open with my finger and couldn't believe my eyes. It read: **'They were warned! *One down!*** I thought holy hell, whose dead now? I looked for the AP guy. It was like he vanished into thin air. Where in the blazed did he go?

Didn't have to wait long for the answer of who was the "one down", my cell phone started vibrating. It was Sunday.

"Reed, Governor Gaker was shot about fifteen minutes ago as he was walking with his wife and family to his limousine. They were going to church. His security bodyguards immediately scoured the area for the shooter.

"He was taken out with a clean hit to the forehead. It probably was a long-range sniper rifle. The FBI boys are taking the matter over and Domel will more than likely be calling me within the hour with some kind of report. "

"Sunday, how coincidental. I have a message in my hand that I received just minutes ago. I'll read it, 'They were warned! One down!' It was delivered to me via an AP messenger, at least he was dressed like one. I made the mistake of being too curious and opened the sealed envelope without caring to get a good look at the guy. After reading the message, I looked to see where he went and there was no sign of him.

"I'll send this message, after I photo copy it, to the FBI lab. But, I doubt whether it will tell us anything. This group isn't about to slip-up now. It still spooks me on how they can respond so quickly. It's like they anticipate everyone's moves, or just maybe they are ready for any contingency that might happen."

"Reed, it's any ones guess. We're dealing with some very smart cookies. I'll follow through and catch up with you later."

My phone vibrated again this time it was President Stone. He asked if I knew what has happened and I related to him what took place up until his call. We agreed that I should meet him in the Situation Room as soon as possible.

On the way, I couldn't help thinking about the fear this must be putting into all the Governor's minds. Ratification will certainly move along very quickly from this point on. Any one whom might have had second thoughts about vetoing the laws will want them passed within the coming week. All State legislatures will be on it bright and early tomorrow morning. That's Monday May 19th, so by Friday May 23rd all the laws should be ratified. Hopefully in the meantime no one else gets blasted.

At least this new assassination will pull the attention away from the Muslim terrorist group, ISIS and their constant intimation efforts to provoke the U.S. into an all-out war in Iraq. If it was up to me, I'd be using unmanned aerial vehicles (UMV's) right now against ISIS when they cross the imaginary border into Syria. ISIS wasn't satisfied with controlling Mosul, it had to eliminate the border between Iraq and Syria.

Drones, malleable robots (soft material robots), insect-size air force are but a few of the myriad futuristic war-fighting creations currently being developed with government funding. Some of these newly developed creations will be in use by our military within five years.

The Middle East is a ticking time bomb for world war number three. This country has stuck its neck out so far it just could get it chopped off. And for what, money, yeah just money and the love of war because it generated billions of dollars for the elite.

It chills me to think that if Russia and China really renewed their friendship and try what Adolph Hitter attempted---this country would be in deep do-do. That's why I got a personal hard-on for the news media's. Especially, Fox News (Adelaide News), which in really reports half-truths. In fact, Murdoch himself said that Fox news can no longer be "fair and balanced" because the newspaper baron openly claimed that it is not. Even one of Fox News pet song-birds revealed, and I quote, "Distortions are how some people (meaning himself) make a living."

What should be told to the America's citizens is that the person, whomever, that sits in the Oval Office can't do a damn blasted thing about stopping a war because the United States is the largest armament dealer in the world.

Arms sales exceeded 400 hundred billion dollars in 2010, and America's Lockheed Martin (35.7 billion) is on the top of a list of 44 companies in this country. These figures come from the Stockholm International Peace Research Institute (SIPRI). They list the top 100 companies selling military armament: U.S with 75 ranks # 1 / Russia with19 ranks # 2 / Japan with 16 ranks # 3 / U. K. with 13 ranks # 4 / Italy with 12 ranks # 5 / Germany. India, and Turkey with 11 each rank # 6 South Korea with 10 ranks # 7. The rest of the 320 plus companies have between 9 and 1 military armament companies. These company's sell military vehicles, tanks, airplanes, missiles, hand and long ranges guns, bombs, land mines, and any other conceivable weaponry for fighting wars.

24/7 Wall Street knows that war is the parent of armies, which are the root of debt and taxes for the citizens of America. This country's budget is unaffected by a bad economy, in fact, they profit more because a bad economy keeps people thinking about how bad it is for them and not the conflicts that the rich elite quietly slip through Congress.

I know because I've seen the Wall Street's stock reports for the top ten companies that make the most profit from war: Lockheed Martin (NYSE-LMT), BAE Systems (NYSE-BAES.L), Boeing (NYSE-BA), Northrop Grumman (NYSE NOC), General Dynamics (NYSE-GD), are the top five. It's easy to see the reasons why they are the top armament sellers with these Middle East countries at war: Iraq, Iran, Egypt, Syria, Israel, Palestine, Turkey, Lebanon, along with Ukraine, and Russia.

In my very private opinion America's rich elite are at the base core of war (s) so they can keep pulling money out of the taxpayer's income trough. Their economy is safe and sound, but not so for the poor working slob. They're struggling in a below average minimum wage. Every time an increase for it comes up before congress it's defeated. Well, maybe help is on its way with these new laws. If the United States can cut-off ISSIL's financing through the sale of the oil that is confiscated and smuggled into Turkey, that would certain end that crisis.

The energy minister in Turkey denies claims that Turkey purchases smuggled oil from all militant groups and sells it through its black-market. Oil smuggling has long been an issue both from Iraq and Syria, especially after the first Iraqi war when a global ban on oil shipments from Iraq was imposed. Alas, doing that would drag the CIA and Wall Street through its murky oil trail and that wouldn't set too well with quite a few Senators. It could bring on a financial Pearl Harbor.

SITUATION ROOM MEETING

Arriving at the Situation Room met Sunday and Domel. Entering, I could see Vice-President Thorne, Attorney General Todd Gettem, the NEA's head, Edwin Cage and one whom I didn't expect, Joyce Web the National Governors Association Communications Director. I wondered why?

Before I could form an opinion the President spoke, "Gentlemen, my special guest today is the Director of the National Governor's Association, Joyce Web. She is present to day to comment about the attitudes of the State Governor's that were prior to our present crisis. I believe she is acquainted with all of you, so there is no need for the customary introductions. Miss Web you have the floor."

"Mr. President and gentlemen let me begin by stepping back in time. In 1964, the Republican nominee for the presidency, Barry Goldwater actually ran on an anti-government platform. His belief was not to improve the government but to shrink it. He, as you all know, didn't get elected but his ideology became the focal point of the Republican Party.

"The Republican Party took advantage of the still small, but growing public dislike for its government by using rhetoric about the failure of the Vietnam War and the Watergate scandal. These coupled with a failing economy helped to convince a small majority of the people that government was bad.

"When Ronald Regan got elected his era proved to be the beginning of a movement funded by certain conservative and powerful anti-government wealthy elite to eliminate the federal government. During his presidency a propaganda campaign to convince the people of this country that, in Regan's own words, 'Government isn't the solution; it is the problem.' They tried to put across the idea that this nation would be better off if the federal government just disappeared. Politics began to change here in D.C. It became infiltrated with crooked politicians in almost all of the late President Franklin Roosevelt New Deal programs. Scandals broke out and people started to mistrust their own government.

"The political right anti-government coalition was campaigning to demonize government and shrink it dramatically. Regan's words were actually spoken during his inaugural speech on January 20th of 1981.

"Today there new title is 'Class Warfare' which is a movement, by elected republican governors, to convince the voters to reduce government, curtail business regulations, and unleash the free market system by systematically taking various rights away from them.

"The assassination attacks of Senators and other officials didn't seem to faze these right wing governors until one of their own was gunned down. The demands of the **Righteous Freedom Group,** which is the name newspaper journalism have begun to call these assassins, will be met by the end of this coming week.

"Naturally, they are all worried about this year's up-coming gubernatorial elections in November. There are thirty-six states which be effected by the new term demands and there is a certain amount of confusion as to how it will effect each of them. They have already served four years, but the unanswered question is will they be able to serve two more years or are they out as of the end of their term?"

The President interrupted by saying, "Excuse me Miss Web, but I believe that Section 5 of S.J.RES. 1 states that all present elected officials will finish out their present term and shall not seek re-election. What will be necessary is to abide by S.J.RES. 2 which states that the campaigning time period will begin no sooner than six months prior to the day of the casting of votes/ballads and will cease that day thereof.

"So, these officials are definitely out of office and can't run for re-election. Still, I believe their terms can be extended for a brief, and I do mean brief, time period, until new nominees will have to be selected and a date to begin to campaign will have to be set. Congress will have to act on that issue. This could take from six months to a year, but I'm sure that this demand group is will understand the situation and allow Congress to proceed along those lines. Now, please continue Miss Web."

"Therein lies another Governor's problem. The voting rights of each state's citizens are under attack in a great many states. Each state will have to gear-up to create and issue picture I.D. voters cards. This will also take time." She paused and looked at the President.

"Miss Web, I will address that issue carefully and make a public statement about my decision. Now, continue."

"My point to my past history facts is I believe that this present crisis has been masterminded by the one percent ultra-wealthy elite and they are in control of these assassinations. Each of the joint resolutions are geared to reduce government and its spending through term limits, salary reductions, no pensions, less representatives, elimination of congressional health benefits, disbanding of the Electoral College and no salaries or, bonuses for committee work and a new monetary system. Plus, I'm sure there will be more demands on the horizon.

"As I see it, the passing of these laws will definitely reduce the government in size and its spending. But, all of this won't change the real problem with America's middle-class, because the real problems lies within one extremely wealthy family.

"Again let's take a brief walk back in time. Prior to the year 2000 (pre-Bush) this wealthy family's banking empire controlled all of the money in the 165 or so countries on this planet except for seven countries: Afghanistan, Iraq, Iran, Libya, Sudan, Cuba, and North Korea. In 2003, (after the 9/11 attack and invasion of Iraq & Afghanistan) Iran, Libya, Sudan, Cuba and North Korea were the only ones not controlled by the family's banking empire.

By 2011, only Iran, Cuba and North Korea were left. Now, the most desired prize is the Central Bank of the Islamic Republic of Iran. Thusly, the present ISIS and ISIL crisis in Iraq and Syria, is taking place to force America to re-enter with ground troops Iraq. This could conceivable lead us into a war with Iran.

"Let me quote from a speech of the Malaysian Prime Minister Mahathir Mohamed about Israel's absolute desire for the water and oil rights in Iraq, 'Jews rule the world by proxy. They get others to fight and die for them.' It think you all get the drift and meaning of that statement.

"To back up that statement, on October 3rd, Israel Prime Minister, Ariel Sharon, said to an Ashkenazi Jew, Shimon Peres, as reported on Kol Yisrael radio, 'Every time we do something you tell me America will do this and will do that....I want to tell you something very clear, don't worry about American pressure on Israel. We, the Jewish people, control America, and the Americans know it.'

"That statement is quite sad, but very true. Let me bring to your attention that in 1948, President Truman made Israel a sovereign state at the request of the patriarch of this wealthy banking family. It was rumored that the family donated two million dollars to his campaign. This banking family's method of gaining control is quite simple, get a country's corrupt politicians to accept massive loans, which they can never repay, and thusly are in debt to them. If a leader, dictator or president refuses to accept the loan, he, she is usually ousted or assassinated. And if that fails, a U.S. invasions usually follows and when the dust settles a usury-based bank is established.

"Mr. President, am I getting too lengthy in my explanation?"

"No Miss Web, please continue."

"To back up my previous statement of how this corrupt banking family's system works, I have to get back into the facts of the history of the assassinated Presidents of America.

"First we had Abraham Lincoln, the 16th President (1861-1865) who prevented this banking family's involvement in financing the Civil War. Lincoln foiled the bankers by refusing loans at 24 to 36 percent interest to finance the war, instead he funding the government with U.S. Notes called 'Greenbacks' that did not accrue interest and did not have to be paid back to any bank.

"But, that didn't stop this greedy banking family. Their agent Salmon P. Chasse, the Treasury Secretary of the United States created and push through Congress the National Banking Act bill in 1864. This bill created a federally chartered central bank and gave it the power to issue U.S. Bank Notes. Lincoln successfully fought against the central bank to limit their power of issuing notes for just the war years and this became the most popular theory behind his assassination (April 15, 1865).

"Then there was Andrew Jackson, who in early January of 1835 declared his opposition toward bankers by calling them 'vipers' and vetoed the renewal of the charter for the Bank of the United States. Soon after an English man named Richard Lawrence attempted to assassinate him. No proof was ever connected to a bank conspiracy. But Jackson did tell his Vice-President Martin Van Buren, 'The bank, Mr. Van Buren, is trying to kill me.'

"President Zachary Taylor (1849-1850) said before he died after eating a bowl of cherries and milk, 'The idea of a national bank is dead, and will not be revived in my time.' It was suspected arsenic poison did the job.

"James Buchanan (1857-1861) and thirty-seven other were poisoned at a banquet. Buchanan was the only survivor. He also was openly and strongly opposed to privately owned banking systems.

"President Garfield (1881-1881) was also anti-central banks which is related in a speech four months prior to being shot on July 2, 1881, by Charles Guiteau in the Sixth Street railroad station in Washington, DC. He died in bed of his wound infections in a New Jersey Oceanside cottage, on September 19, 1881.

"Following Garfield there was President William McKinley (1897-1901), and in 1975, an attempt on President Gerald Ford's life. If Ford was assassinated that would have meant Vice-President Nelson Rockefeller, a member of the international bankers would have been president.

"Of course, you all are aware of President J. F. Kennedy's Executive Order 11110 which was returning the privilege of printing and coining money back to the United States Government and ousting the Federal Reserve System. He was also assassinated in 1963.

"Others who also championed revealing the interest usury robbery of the tax payers' money by the FEDs met with rather suspicious or coincidental deaths: Congressman Larry P. McDonald, Senator John Heinz and former Senator John Tower were all killed in plane crash as was J.F k's son John Jr. All very strange coincidences, it would seem.

"Mr. President and gentlemen, in conclusion, I strongly believe that whomever is responsible for the assassinations has been organized and is being funded by the ***money power*** people and that is why no clues or anything leading to their identity has been found. And, as far as the death of Jarvis Cove, he was just collateral damage.

"Finally, the ***money power*** people, or the famous London banking family headed by the great, great, great grandson of Mayer Amschel Rothschild Lord Evelyn Robert, want and will do anything possible to gain global control **(New World Order)** and return all countries into a feudal system. Thank you Mr. President and gentlemen for your time and ears.

"And as a post script, remember, in 1948, Harry S. Truman was influenced by this famous banking family, who owned the territory in which Israel sits upon, to recognize Israel's territory as a Zionist not Jewish territory and to become a sovereign state. The famous London banking family has been doing ***their thing*** for over 200 years and are probably worth in liquid assets in the neighborhood of $350 trillion bananas in a bunch according to Credit Suisse."

There was silence in the room for a few seconds and then the President Stone spoke, "Thank you Miss Web for your theory and pointing out a great many facts that some of us might not have been unaware of."

The President looked around the room waiting for someone else to speak. It was Sunday who broke the silence.

"An extremely fine explanation of a conspiracy theory pertaining to who wants to control the wealth of the world. There is no doubt in any one's mind that's seated in this room who the banking family that you were referring to is throughout your comments.

"The past patriarch of this family, in 1812, gained control of the British economy and they are using their money magic on the third world countries and this country to gain their control. As you stated, they have had over 200 hundred years to practice their special brand of financial witchcraft and have employed unspeakable methods to achieve them.

"Yes, Miss Web, I believe that the money powers on this planet are using everything within their power to control every country's wealth and populations. But, take into consideration this particular banking family. Their financial magical trick bag controls the three largest U.S. media networks and many other aspects of the news industry. And, it doesn't stop there, their funding power has control of the depopulation advocacy groups and codex alimentarius (Latin for **FOOD CODE).**

"The Codex Alimentarius Commission, in 2002, covertly surrendered its role as a guardian of the people's health. Its new code is to increase the profits of the giant global corporations in the food, drug and chemical businesses while controlling the world through ***FOOD.*** Their wish in sicknesses and diseases, is not to cure, but only treat them to maintain a constant flow of prescription money.

"The only way to stop the rich elite (1%) from taking complete control of this country is in the voting power of the people. That's why I think this assassination group or the newspaper title 'R*ighteous Freedom Group'* has shown its strength through killing and fear. After all, what motivates people the most---fear, that's what!

"Sure, we have problems with immigration, import and export taxes, street drugs, corporation subsidies, gun control, social entitlement programs, this country's educational system, credit card limits and their usury interest rates by banks, but they can all be corrected by electing the politicians who will represent the people not big business.

"That's why I personal believe in, but adamantly do not condone the actions of this murderous group, their demands to change our government. Elected politicians have for more than five decades feathered their unholy beds at the expense of the tax payers without regard to their welfare. They have allowed themselves to be bought and in return have bowed to the wishes of the money donators.

"As far as I'm concerned, this group has given this country a second chance to get itself on the right path to a real government by the people and for the people. I want to be heard and recorded that Mr. Domel and myself are and will use every facility, electronic equipment and manpower to do everything in our power to apprehend these assassins. Then, we will leave the due process of the law to Mr. Gettem, the District Attorney.

"Well, I've said my piece. I yield the floor."

"Thank you Mr. Sunday. Any one else ready and willing to commit to the reasoning of this crisis?"

"Yes, Mr. President I am." General Josh White said as he stood up.

"Military, yes military power is what this country needs. This ISIL situation in Iraq and Syria had weakened your popularity in the eyes of not only this country but the whole world. These beheadings and the ISIS badgering us to **'put boots on the ground'** in Iraq is very dangerous to this country's military power. All your words of getting them fall upon deaf ears of the military men of this country. Especially, those who are mentally disturbed and those that have missing arms and legs.

"We have to stop lying to the citizens of this country and tell them the truth about why there are terrorist groups throughout the Middle-East. Miss Web is absolutely right. It's all over oil and control of those oil rich countries. Ever since George H.W. Bush did to get even with the family al-Sabah of Kuwait for their over-production of oil in 1991, the Persian Gulf War the Middle-East has remained a **'hot box'**. **Oh, by the way, the oil well fires were set by Americans, not the Iraqi.** That came out in a 2003 investigation.

"I would be standing here for at least eight hours trying to explain that war over oil and there is no need for that. My reason and fear is that if Russia and China ever decide to hook-up and take on the United States in war we won't win.

"This country no longer has the blood and guts citizens of the WWII days. They're dying off each year and all this country has today is a couple of generations of 'soft bellied' citizens. They want every dam electronic toy there is to occupy their minds and could care less about **'the other guy'.** They believe the newscasters lies about everything. They're broke and in debt up too their ears to the top twelve banks. They don't save any money because they can make even enough to pay rent, car payments, raise a family and enjoy a little free time.

"The banking industry has completed their first step of bring the United States into a feudal country dominated by the rich elite. All of the demands that are going to be passed will take time to bring our government around to protecting and helping its citizens. The confusion and chaos of this crisis is ripe for an attack on the United States. Sure, I realize that we have a very large arsenal of war weapons, but so does China and Russia.

"What this country needs to prevent this weakness is a mandatory draft system. There are approximately three and one-half million students expected to graduate this coming June. My proposal is to have each and every one of them, male and female, serve an eighteen month period in the various military services of this country. Disciplined and trained for a possible war at any time. We have almost two million allied forces standing ready right now and millions in the National Guard and State Militias. America must be prepared at any time to retaliate an attack. And, gentlemen, it won't be on the ground, but by robotic planes and missiles. The United States is no longer out of the reach of war on its soil."

THE PRESIDENT LAYS IT ON THE LINE

As General White was about to continue, President Stone stood up and interrupted him saying; "Gentlemen and of course Miss Web, this type of conversation is getting us nowhere. We are six months away from mid-term elections for both houses. And, as we all know mid-term elections are not a top priority of the working middle class. They tend to not show up at the polls. The Republicans know this because of their success in 2010 mid-term elections, and will spend hundreds of millions dollars getting as many seats as they can to control both of the houses. Assassination demands or not, they will be doing their hobnobbery to make the Democratic opposition look like assholes. Pardon my French. So, we really need to rush the Amendment demands into law ASAP.

"We only have a very short window in time to stop further bloodshed. If they grab control of both houses it's a sure bet they'd attempt to dismantle my Health-care program by not funding parts of it, introduce their own immigration laws to grab the credit of the Hispanic voter, start an underground way to un-do these new laws, approve the Keystone pipeline, push aside those who are blocking the tar-sands movement, and of course, create more obstacles for democratic voters.

"Voting must be a very critical part of this country's survival, however, the present two-party system doesn't fit well if a nation isn't to be allowed to express their true intentions via the voting process for governing this country. The will of the one percent to have an oligarchy form of government is precisely what the ***Pilgrims at the Plymouth Colony*** were governed by. Do we want to return to having no government to protect the people, just a handful of ultra- rich SOB?

"The real honest expression of the citizens of this country comes from the grassroots level who will help to stop all the mighty wishes of those who want a ***New World Order.*** To be quite blunt about it, we must destroy our present ***clusterfuckery*** called a ***Democracy and build a new Republic*** type of government.

"Remember, a Republic form of government is when the power is in the hands of the people who elect representatives to respond to the majority people's wishes. Sovereignty must rest with the people of a nation and not a few elite rich families.

"Now, we will adjourn so each of us can do our part to save this county and stop any further killings from these assassins. I'll be on hand for all results, questions or whatever."

CHAPTER SEVEN
MID-TERM ELECTIONS

The following weeks turned into months and before long it was autumn and the mid-term elections battles were in full bloom. The Monkey Cage predictions reported that the Democrats would be massacred with the Republicans getting Congressional control in twenty-one states and the Democrats fourteen out of the thirty-five state elections. It proved to be true.

All of the newscasters reported the reason being that the Democrats didn't put forward a strong message of how they were going to improve the economy. Well, that's a lot of bull crap. The real reason was the dollars spent blasting President Rackston Stone. After all, he's the party leader and that's who gets all the heat. Besides, he's of color.

It's very hard to believe that the American public still don't realize that the President is only one man and that he doesn't have a magic wand to wave over every stinkin' lousy problem in this country. No man is an island. It takes a united and un-bound Congress to pass the right laws to govern this country.

But, I guess the future of this country will lie in the hands of the "*Newbies"* in both houses. Especially after yesterday's headlines;

FINALLY MESSAGE—ULTIMATUM!

Jim-jam, holy Sam, it makes me shake all over reading it,

**WE BROUGHT THEM DOWN
AND YOU LEARNED FEAR,
DON'T ALLOW THEM ARISE
OR, YOU AGAIN FROM US WILL HEAR!**

The message was found in the mailroom of the Washington Post on a blood stained piece of paper lying on the floor. Lab results of the blood---chicken, and no fingerprints. **I wonder if the chicken blood had any special meaning. Well, I guess we all have to wait and see?**

An additional note from the author:

The message of this novel strongly suggests the belief in a quote from John Milton who was born in 1608 and became a well-to-do lawyer, private banker, poet and a civil servant for the Commonwealth of England.

"The Truth will always prevail in a free-thinking, uncensored society."

And, George Washington tossed in his two cents worth with:

"Truth will ultimately prevail where there is pains taken to bring it to light."

There have been several other novels written about this subject and if a reader wishes to seek other views they are available on Amazon.

P.S. Another question begs to be answered, "Why are a great percentage of police departments throughout the United States being supplied with Army military armored equipment?

Now, the powers to be have our complete military forces consisting of the U. S. Army, Navy, Marines, Air Force, the National Guard, Border Patrol, State Police, City Police Departments, and each State Governor's private militia?

I wonder what is on the horizon for future generations.

End---Who can guess?

December 5th, 2014